HARRIET TUBMAN

Recent Titles in Greenwood Biographies

HARRIET TUBMAN

A Biography

James A. McGowan and William C. Kashatus

GREENWOOD BIOGRAPHIES

GREENWOOD

AN IMPRINT OF ABC-CLIO, LLC
Santa Barbara, California • Denver, Colorado • Oxford, England

Copyright 2011 by ABC-CLIO, LLC

All rights reserved. No part of this publication may be reproduced, stored in a retrieval system, or transmitted, in any form or by any means, electronic, mechanical, photocopying, recording, or otherwise, except for the inclusion of brief quotations in a review, without prior permission in writing from the publisher.

Library of Congress Cataloging-in-Publication Data

McGowan, James A.
   Harriet Tubman : a biography / James A. McGowan and William C. Kashatus. — Greenwood biographies
       p. cm.
   Includes bibliographical references and index.
   ISBN 978-0-313-34881-5 (hard copy : acid-free paper) —
ISBN 978-0-313-34882-2 (ebook)
   1. Tubman, Harriet, 1820?–1913. 2. Slaves—United States—Biography.
   3. African American women—Biography. I. Kashatus, William C.,
1959– II. Title.
   E444.T82M34   2011
   973.7'115092—dc22
   [B]   2010042697

ISBN: 978-0-313-34881-5
EISBN: 978-0-313-34882-2

15 14 13 12 11   1 2 3 4 5

This book is also available on the World Wide Web as an eBook.
Visit www.abc-clio.com for details.

Greenwood
An Imprint of ABC-CLIO, LLC

ABC-CLIO, LLC
130 Cremona Drive, P.O. Box 1911
Santa Barbara, California 93116-1911

This book is printed on acid-free paper (∞)

Manufactured in the United States of America

*For James and Lois Horton, whose
scholarship and examples have inspired a new generation
of African American historians, both black and white.*

CONTENTS

SERIES FOREWORD

In response to high school and public library needs, Greenwood developed this distinguished series of full-length biographies specifically for student use. Prepared by field experts and professionals, these engaging biographies are tailored for high school students who need challenging yet accessible biographies. Ideal for secondary school assignments, the length, format and subject areas are designed to meet educators' requirements and students' interests.

Greenwood offers an extensive selection of biographies spanning all curriculum related subject areas including social studies, the sciences, literature and the arts, history and politics, as well as popular culture, covering public figures and famous personalities from all time periods and backgrounds, both historic and contemporary, who have made an impact on American and/or world culture. Greenwood biographies were chosen based on comprehensive feedback from librarians and educators. Consideration was given to both curriculum relevance and inherent interest. The result is an intriguing mix of the well known and the unexpected, the saints and sinners from long-ago history and contemporary pop culture. Readers will find a wide array of subject choices from fascinating crime figures like Al Capone to inspiring pioneers like Margaret

Mead, from the greatest minds of our time like Stephen Hawking to the most amazing success stories of our day like J. K. Rowling.

While the emphasis is on fact, not glorification, the books are meant to be fun to read. Each volume provides in-depth information about the subject's life from birth through childhood, the teen years, and adulthood. A thorough account relates family background and education, traces personal and professional influences, and explores struggles, accomplishments, and contributions. A timeline highlights the most significant life events against a historical perspective. Bibliographies supplement the reference value of each volume.

INTRODUCTION

In the spring of 1860, Harriet Tubman set out from her home in Auburn, New York, for Boston where she planned to attend an antislavery conference. During the trip, the petite, five-foot-tall black abolitionist stopped at Troy to visit a cousin. No sooner had she arrived in town that she learned of the arrest of a 30-year-old fugitive slave, Charles Nalle.

Nalle had escaped from his owner, Blooker Hansborough of Culpepper County, Virginia, two years earlier. He settled in the small town of Sand Lake, about twelve miles south of Troy, where he found employment as a coachman for a prominent family. When Hansborough discovered that his runaway slave was living in upstate New York, he enlisted the help of a slave catcher, H. W. Averill, to locate and return him to Virginia.

On the morning of April 27, Nalle was arrested in downtown Troy by U.S. deputy marshal Henry J. Wall and taken to the local magistrate, Miles Beach. Examining the legal documents presented by Averill, Beach determined that Nalle was indeed the property of the Virginia planter and ordered that he be returned to his master.

By two o'clock in the afternoon, an unruly crowd of black and white residents gathered outside the magistrate's office in the Mutual Bank

Building at the corner of First and State Streets. They could see the tall, light-complexioned Nalle standing in front of a second-story window gazing at the crowd, desperate for help. Some demanded that he be freed. Others offered to raise $1,200 to purchase his freedom. Still others appealed for law and order.

When Tubman arrived at the scene, a great cheer erupted among the blacks. "There is Moses!" they exclaimed, referring to Tubman's biblical nickname. "As long as she is here, [Nalle] is safe!" Wrapped in a shawl and carrying a food basket, Tubman played the role of a feeble old woman to gain entry to the magistrate's chamber. She entered the building and tried to get to the second floor, but the stairway was jammed with people. Officers attempted to clear the way for their prisoner. Tubman, realizing the necessity for rescue, ordered some small boys to go outside and cry, "Fire!"

A path immediately cleared and the officers descended the staircase with Nalle, who was shackled hand and foot. Once they were outside, Tubman shouted to the black spectators: "Here he comes—take him!"

The crowd closed ranks around the officers and their prisoner. Tubman muscled her way into the fray, seizing one officer and pulling him down as Nalle broke free. Wrapping her arms around the runaway, she ordered the mob: "Drag us out! Drag him to the river! Drown him, but don't let them have him!"

Tubman and Nalle were pushed to the ground. While lying there, the shrewd abolitionist tore off her sunbonnet and tied it on the head of the fugitive. When Nalle rose to his feet only his head could be seen. Amid the surging mass of people, he could no longer be recognized.

Again and again, the mob knocked them down. Nalle's shackled wrists were bleeding. Tubman's clothes were torn and her shoes pulled from her feet. But she never loosened her grasp of the fugitive until she led him to the river where he tumbled into a wooden skiff and was rowed to the other side. Authorities were lying in wait on the opposite bank and they took Nalle back into custody. Refusing to be outdone, nearly four hundred abolitionists, determined to protect the fugitive, boarded a ferry and crossed the river. Once again, Tubman led the charge.

She organized her antislavery troops into a human battering ram and stormed the building where Nalle was taken. When the abolitionists who broke through the door of the judge's office were stricken down,

Tubman and several other women rushed over the bodies, seized Nalle, and placed him in a wagon. Nalle was hurried out of town, successfully eluding a return to slavery.[1]

Harriet Tubman, born a slave on Maryland's Eastern Shore, was the best-known African-American female abolitionist in antebellum America. Since she was an illiterate black woman, her success seemed unlikely. Yet Tubman rose to prominence within a reform movement dominated by highly educated, middle-class white men. The key to her success was her involvement on the secret—and illegal—network of antislavery activists known as the Underground Railroad. On 13 separate occasions, Tubman braved unimaginable dangers to assist some 70 escaping slaves to freedom in the North.[2] On several occasions she rescued mothers and their children, drugging infants with laudanum to prevent their crying from revealing her hiding places. Tubman carried a revolver and was not afraid to use it against a determined slave catcher or even a frightened runaway who had second thoughts about escape.[3] Her exploits earned her the nickname "Moses," after the Old Testament prophet who led the Hebrews out of bondage.[4] During the Civil War, Tubman shifted her efforts to serving the Union Army. She was a nurse for soldiers suffering from dysentery at Port Royal, South Carolina, and later served as an armed scout and spy.[5] Tubman's involvement as a soldier was even more impressive. Guiding federal troops up the Combahee River, she led an armed expedition to capture plantations in South Carolina and liberated an estimated 750 slaves. In so doing, she became the first woman to lead a military expedition in an American war.[6]

After the Civil War, Tubman retired to the family home in Auburn, New York, where she cared for her aging parents.[7] She was also involved in the women's suffrage movement until poor health forced her to enter a home for elderly African Americans she had helped establish years earlier.[8] It was there that she passed away on March 10, 1913.

Harriet Tubman was an American icon even before her death, brought to prominence largely by contemporary biographers. Franklin B. Sanborn, an abolitionist newspaper editor, was the first to chronicle her Underground Railroad exploits in a biographical sketch that appeared in the *Boston Commonwealth* as early as 1863.[9] Two years later, Ednah Dow Cheney celebrated Tubman as "the most remarkable woman of this age" having "performed more wonderful deeds by the native power of her own spirit than any other."[10] A more detailed biography was published in 1869 by Sarah H. Bradford. Titled *Scenes in the Life of Harriet Tubman*, Bradford's work emphasized Tubman's dual importance as both an Underground Railroad agent and an early women's rights advocate. The biography was heavily supplemented with testimonials of Harriet's reformer friends and with newspaper accounts of her daring rescues.[11] Bradford expanded her initial treatment in 1886 with a revised biography titled *Harriet Tubman: The Moses of Her People*.[12]

Since all of these biographies were written by friends and admirers—qualities that prevented an objective analysis—Tubman's life and achievements were embellished. The myths were replicated in several highly dramatized children's versions that followed. In fact, Tubman is the subject of more children's books than any other African American figure. Celebrated as a race heroine in the early 20th century by women's suffragists, Tubman's example also inspired later generations of African Americans engaged in the struggle for civil rights. Public statues were erected bearing her likeness. The United States Maritime Commission named its first Liberty ship for her, and the U.S. Postal Service issued a stamp in her honor. Dozens of schools, streets, and buildings across the country were dedicated to her. Tubman's home in Auburn, New York, and a museum in Cambridge, Maryland, serve as monuments to her life.[13] Her image has become so romanticized that it is difficult to separate the myth from the reality. *Harriet Tubman: A Biography* goes beyond the mythology of this African American icon by offering an objective portrait of a complex human being who was intelligent and shrewd, but also possessed personal needs and shortcomings. Tubman was self-righteous, insisting that her activities, no matter how controversial, were condoned by God, with whom she claimed to speak on almost a daily basis. As a result, she could be stubborn to a fault when challenged by abolitionists who disagreed with her, though she had to rely on them for refuge and money. Tubman's temper was quick and she was short on patience, especially with runaways who exhibited their fears en route to the North. What's more, questions still exist over whether she kidnapped or rescued from bondage a youngster she claimed was her niece. The uncertainty suggests that Tubman may have longed to have a child of her own. These are among the many controversial issues explored in this book.

This work was begun by James McGowan, who for many years was editor of *The Harriet Tubman Journal*. During the last year of his life, when Jim realized that he would be unable to complete the book, he asked me to become a coauthor. It was a very difficult decision to make. Jim possessed a loyalty to Harriet Tubman that bordered on hero worship. That quality often colored his interpretation of her life and deeds. He spent many years compiling a systematic list of inaccuracies he discovered in the two biographical treatments completed by Sarah Bradford and their replication in subsequent Tubman biographies written by Anne Parrish, Marcy Heidish, and Earl Conrad.[14] So meticulous was his research that more recent Tubman biographers often consulted him during the writing process. Unlike the earlier writers, these were scholars trained in the disciplines of history and women's studies. But if their research on Tubman uncovered a human shortcoming, Jim went to great lengths to disprove it. At the same time, Jim admired their scholarship and often integrated their findings into his own work.

I am much less devoted to Harriet Tubman. Though I view her as a pioneer in both the antislavery and women's rights movements, I am fully aware of her human frailties and less hesitant to identify them. In many respects, Tubman's ability to achieve success in spite of those shortcomings makes her contribution to history even greater than Jim himself might have imagined. But my friendship with Jim and our mutual intellectual commitment to African American history was much stronger than my reservations about completing the book, so I agreed to be a coauthor.

Since our writing styles are noticeably different, I tried to retain the integrity of Jim's interpretation by working with his initial outline of the book as well as his rough drafts of the early chapters. I also consulted the audiotapes I made of our conversations on Harriet Tubman, William Still, Thomas Garrett, and the Underground Railroad for a previous manuscript we coauthored, titled *Angel at Philadelphia: A Study of William Still's Underground Railroad*. While I acknowledge Jim's differences with other more recent Tubman biographers, I place a greater emphasis on maintaining a coherent story line. Since Jim was only able to complete rough drafts of the first four chapters, all of the writing and the research for the remaining chapters are my own. I hope this effort will do justice to Jim's longtime commitment to share his love of Harriet

Tubman with a larger and more diverse audience than his journal reached.

In telling Tubman's story, Jim and I relied on contemporary newspaper accounts, correspondence, and memoirs, as well as recently published Tubman biographies. We've been the beneficiaries of valuable assistance from several individuals, including Catherine Clinton, Larry Gara, Walter Kahoe, Kate Larson, Paul Ressler, Milton Sernett, Margaret Swantko, Frances Taylor, and Elizabeth Williams. Their extensive knowledge of Harriet Tubman's life and labors was invaluable, as was their advice and support.

In addition, we are grateful to Cheryll Woodall for her assistance with the contractual arrangements for this book and to the staff of the Chester County Historical Society for their support, especially Ellen Endslow, Pam Powell and Diane and Laura Rofini. Not only were they wonderful colleagues, but they somehow managed to put up with our constant heckling.

The book is dedicated to historians James and Lois Horton, whom we've known since 2000 when we worked together on one of the nation's first multimedia museum exhibitions on the Underground Railroad at the Chester County Historical Society in West Chester, Pennsylvania. Their scholarship, counsel, and personal encouragement not only resulted in a nationally acclaimed exhibit, but also renewed our appreciation for the necessity of an interracial approach to African American history in general, and the history of the Underground Railroad in particular.

Finally, special thanks are due to our families for indulging us while we spent many years discussing, researching, writing, and speaking about Harriet Tubman and the Underground Railroad.

NOTES

1. See: "Fugitive Slave Rescue," *Troy Whig*: April 28, 1860; and Sarah H. Bradford, *Scenes in the Life of Harriet Tubman* (Auburn, NY: W. J. Moses, 1869), 88.

2. Kate Clifford Larson, *Bound for the Promised Land: Harriet Tubman, Portrait of an American Hero* (New York: Ballantine Books, 2004), xvii. The number of trips Tubman made, as well as the number of slaves

she rescued on the Underground Railroad, are subject to much speculation. Her obituary, which first appeared in Auburn, New York, in March 1913, identifies the totals as "nineteen trips" and "more than four hundred slaves." (See "Death of Aunt Harriet, Moses of Her People," *Auburn Daily Advertiser:* March 11, 1913.) Other accounts, published during the last year of Tubman's life, set the total of slaves rescued by her at 300; see "Harriet Tubman," *American Magazine* 74 (1912): 420–422; and "The Moses of the Negroes," *Literary Digest* 46 (1912): 913–916. But the accuracy of these numbers is doubtful because of the hero worship that Tubman enjoyed in her old age and in the years immediately after her death.

3. Catherine Clinton, *Harriet Tubman: The Road to Freedom* (New York: Little, Brown, 2004), 90–91.

4. Clinton, *Road to Freedom*, 85.

5. Larson, *Bound for the Promised Land*, 204; and Clinton, *Road to Freedom*, 157.

6. Larson, *Bound for the Promised Land*, 239.

7. Larson, *Bound for the Promised Land*, 287; and Clinton, *Road to Freedom*, 192.

8. Larson, *Bound for the Promised Land*, 273–275, 282–288.

9. Franklin B. Sanborn, "Harriet Tubman," *Boston Commonwealth:* July 17, 1863.

10. Ednah Dow Littlehale Cheney, "Moses," *Freedmen's Record:* March 1865.

11. Sarah H. Bradford, *Scenes in the Life of Harriet Tubman* (Auburn, NY: W. J. Moses, 1869).

12. Sarah H. Bradford, *Harriet Tubman: The Moses of Her People* (1886; reprint, Secaucus, NJ: Citadel Press, 1961).

13. Milton C. Sernett, *Harriet Tubman: Myth, Memory, and History* (Durham, NC: Duke University Press, 2007), 21–40.

14. See James A. McGowan, *Harriet Tubman Journal* 1, no. 2 (August 1993); 2, no. 1 (January 1994); and 3, no. 2 (August 1995).

TIMELINE: EVENTS IN THE LIFE OF HARRIET TUBMAN

ca. 1820	Born Araminta "Minty" Ross in Dorchester County, Maryland, to Harriet "Rit" Green and Ben Ross, probably in February or March.
March 2, 1824	Edward Brodess, Minty's owner, marries Eliza Ann Keene. Minty and the rest of her family are separated from their father and moved to Brodess's plantation.
1826	Hired out to various Dorchester County farms to work as nursemaid and laborer.
1834	Suffers head injury while helping a slave escape.
1844	Marries John Tubman, a free black man.
September 17, 1849	Escapes from bondage with her brothers after the death of Edward Brodess. But brothers have second thoughts and force her to return with them to the Brodess plantation. One month later, Harriet runs away by herself, using the Underground Railroad, and resettles at Philadelphia.

December 1850	Conducts first rescue mission by helping her niece Kessiah and her children escape.
December 1851	Guides a group of 11 fugitives north on the Underground Railroad and crosses the Canadian border for the first time.
1852	Makes second trip on the Underground Railroad to persuade her husband to join her in Philadelphia. She discovers that he is happily remarried and prefers to remain in Maryland.
May–July 1857	Rescues her mother, Harriet "Rit" Green, and father, Ben Ross, on the Underground Railroad, and guides them to Canada.
April 1858	Meets abolitionist John Brown.
1859	Purchases a small plot of land in Auburn, New York, for $1,200 from United States Senator William H. Seward, an abolitionist. Builds a house on the land that becomes a haven for family and friends.
1860	Conducts her final rescue mission on the Underground Railroad.
1862	Serves as a nurse for soldiers suffering from dysentery at Port Royal, South Carolina.
June 1, 1863	Assists Union Colonel James Montgomery and his troops on raids of plantations along the Combahee River in South Carolina.
1865	Returns to Auburn, New York.
September 30, 1867	Husband John Tubman is murdered in Cambridge, Maryland.
December 1868	Sarah Bradford publishes *Scenes in the Life of Harriet Tubman*, the first biographical treatment of the Underground Railroad heroine.
March 18, 1869	Marries Civil War veteran Nelson Davis at Auburn, New York.
1886	A new edition of Tubman's biography, *Moses of Her People*, is published by Sarah Bradford.
October 18, 1888	Second husband Nelson Davis dies.

1896	Speaks at charter meeting of the National Federation of Afro-American Women; purchases land to build a home for elderly and sick African Americans.
June 23, 1908	Opening of the Harriet Tubman Home by the African Methodist Episcopal Zion Church, Auburn, New York.
March 10, 1913	Dies at Auburn, New York.
March 13, 1913	Buried with military honors at Fort Hill Cemetery, Auburn, New York.

Chapter 1

MINTY, 1820–1840

Maryland's Eastern Shore lies on a peninsula situated between the Atlantic Coastal Plain and the Chesapeake Bay. Because the states of Delaware, Maryland, and Virginia hold mutual title to the area, it is known as the Delmarva Peninsula. But Maryland is more closely identified with the land mass because of the state's central location on it.

Of Maryland's Eastern Shore counties, Dorchester is the most picturesque. Bounded by the Choptank River to the north, and the Nanticoke to the south and east, the county extends from the Chesapeake Bay to the Delaware state line and consists of some 400,000 acres. Deer, Canadian geese, black ducks, and mallards are plentiful in the surrounding wetlands, and the forests are rich in oak, hickory, pine, walnut, and sweet gum. Dorchester County is also blessed with an extensive network of rivers and creeks, offering access to trade and preferable sites for shipbuilding. A mild but humid climate produces hot summers and cool winters, which is ideal for growing tobacco, the earliest cash crop of Maryland's economy. At the same time, tobacco growing is labor—intensive. It demands rich, fertile soil and constant attention. And, to be most profitable, tobacco farming must be completed by slaves.

Map of Dorchester County, Maryland, ca. 1800–1860. (Courtesy of Michael Dolan)

The first African slaves arrived in Maryland in 1642, just eight years after Lord Baltimore established the colony. Since most of the early settlers owned relatively small parcels of land, slaves were not in great demand. Those planters who became affluent relied on other, more profitable enterprises such as land speculation, money lending, trade, manufacturing, and commerce. During the 18th century, slaves were imported to the Eastern Shore in large numbers by a small elite of white merchant-planters and a growing class of yeoman farmers. By the beginning of the 19th century there were more than 38,000 slaves living on Maryland's Eastern Shore, which accounted for 36 percent of the total population of the region.¹ Nearly all the white inhabitants were advocates of slavery, regardless of their economic circumstances. For planters, slaves, though expensive to maintain, were profitable because of their cheap labor. For yeoman farmers and landless whites, the existence of slavery insured their social status since there was a class of people below them. It also fed their ambitions to own slaves, become wealthy, and perhaps even join the planter class.

At the same time, Maryland's Eastern Shore represented a middle ground between slave and free labor. The idiosyncratic nature of the region could be explained, in part, by the presence of a large antislavery population dominated by the Religious Society of Friends (Quakers) and free blacks. Local Friends wrestled with the issue of slavery during the 18th century. Although Quaker theology emphasized the spiritual equality of all human beings, regardless of race, there were those Friends who owned slaves because their personal wealth depended on slave labor. Other Quakers adopted the practice of slaveholding as they increased their property. After 1787, when Baltimore Yearly Meeting, the governing body of Quakers in Maryland, officially condemned slavery and disowned members who owned slaves, many proslavery Friends joined the Methodist Church, which was less rigid in its discipline against slaveholding. Others remained visibly active in the abolitionist movement.

The free black community was in a more precarious position. Many of the region's free blacks had been manumitted by local farmers at the beginning of the 19th century when they abandoned tobacco farming for the growing of cereal grains, such as wheat, which required far less labor and was still highly profitable. But the free blacks lived with the constant fear of being returned to bondage because of the presence of slave catchers like the infamous Patty Cannon, who would readily kidnap a free black person for a bounty. In addition, there were more than 80 slave traders operating on the Eastern Shore who were willing to conspire with Cannon if the price was right. These fears as well as a strong sense of personal obligation to their enslaved brethren motivated the local free black community to dedicate themselves to the abolition of slavery. Together the Quakers and free blacks formed an active Underground Railroad network that wove through Dorchester and neighboring Caroline and Talbot Counties.² It was here, on this middle ground between slavery and freedom, that Harriet Tubman began her life.

Born into slavery around 1820 near Tobacco Stick, Dorchester County, Araminta "Minty" Ross was the daughter of Benjamin Ross and Harriet Green.[3] Her slave parents were owned by different masters. Harriet "Rit" Green was the property of Joseph and Mary Pattison Brodess of Bucktown, Dorchester County, Maryland. Mary Brodess had inherited Rit from her grandfather, Atthow Pattison, with the understanding that Rit and her children would be freed when Rit turned 45. Rit was the daughter of a white man, though his identity is not known. Her mother, Modesty, was a member of the Ashanti tribe, whose leaders fought off British slave traders for more than two centuries. She was probably enslaved as a child in the mid-1700s when she was taken by slave traders from the Gold Coast of West Africa. Modesty might have been sold from the deck of a slave ship on the Chesapeake Bay, or at a slave auction in Oxford, Maryland; eventually she became the property of Atthow Pattison.[4] But her Ashanti origins and the bravery associated with it may have contributed to Araminta's own sense of courage.

Ben Ross was a "full blooded Negro" whose ancestry remains unknown. He was owned by Anthony Thompson, who ran a larger plantation in Madison, Maryland. Ross, a skilled woodsman, supervised Thompson's other slaves who cut and logged timber for the Baltimore shipbuilding industry.[5] Ross met Rit Green sometime after Joseph Brodess's death in 1803. Brodess's widow, Mary, was left with the responsibility to raise their two-year-old son, Edward. In need of a husband to manage the Bucktown farm, she married Thompson, a widower with three sons of his own.[6] The marriage brought the couple's slaves together into one family. Though Benjamin Ross and Rit were unable to marry legally, they considered themselves husband and wife.[7] The arrangement allowed the Ross family to build a home for themselves and their nine children on the Thompson plantation in Madison.[8] Their circumstances changed, however, when Edward Brodess inherited his mother's estate.

Mary Brodess died sometime between 1809 and 1810.[9] Since Edward was just 9 or 10 years old, all of her assets—including slaves and 200 acres of farmland in Bucktown—were managed by her widower, Anthony Thompson. Thompson served as the boy's legal guardian until 1822, when he turned 21. Determined to strike out on his own, Edward, upon inheriting his mother's estate, relocated from Madison to Bucktown. He also took Rit and her children with him, thereby separating the Ross family. On March 2, 1824, he married Eliza Ann Keene, and the couple began their own family.[10]

Brodess's holdings were typical of those in border states like Maryland. Large plantations—those with 200 or more slaves and devoted to raising cotton, sugar, and rice—were a rarity in antebellum America. Those that did exist were located in the Deep South, especially along the banks of the Mississippi River and in the coastal low country of South Carolina and Georgia. By contrast, slaveholdings in the Upper South and the border states were relatively small and constituted more than nine-tenths of rural slaveholdings in antebellum America. Slaveholders in this region were of modest means with small or medium-sized farms. They were "resident masters" who lived on their holdings, took an active interest in running their own estate, and, in many cases, worked alongside their slaves. Many of these slaveholders were tobacco farmers who owned fewer than 10 slaves. Often, the owners were severe in their treatment of the few slaves they owned because their financial income was so closely tied to slave labor. Physical punishment, the selling of family members, and the practice of hiring out slaves in order to earn more income were common among these owners.[11]

Like most small planters, Brodess struggled to increase his income. Although his mother had promised to free Rit and her children in accordance with her grandfather's will, Edward reneged on the agreement and began selling off the children in 1825. The first to go was Mariah, Rit's 16-year-old daughter, followed by the sales of two other daughters, Linah and Soph. While these sales helped to sustain Brodess's own growing family, they left a deep scar within Minty, who watched helplessly as each sister was taken away. She saw the "agonizing expression of their faces, heard their weeping as they turned to take one last look at their home." Then, suddenly, they were "hidden from her sight forever."[12] The sale of her sisters remained with Minty for the rest of her life. "Every time I saw a white man," she admitted, "I was afraid of being carried away."[13]

Devastated by the sale of her daughters, Rit struggled to keep her family together. When a Georgia trader approached Brodess about buying her youngest son, Moses, she threatened to "split his head open" if he tried to take the boy. She then hid Moses among members of the surrounding free black community until Brodess abandoned the sale.[14] Rit's older sons, Ben and Robert, were put to work in the fields. "Where I came from," recalled Ben in later years, "it would make your flesh creep, and your hair stand on end, to know what they did to the slaves."[15] Similarly, Robert contended that Brodess "was not fit to own a dog," and that his wife, Eliza Ann was "very devilish," forcing his siblings to "work hard and fare meagrely" in order to support her in "idleness and luxury."[16] If Brodess was unable to use some of his slaves, he resorted to hiring them out to neighboring farmers. Hiring out slaves, which was a very common practice on the Eastern Shore, could earn as much as $120 per year.[17] Selling slaves and hiring them out were only two of the horrific practices masters employed to exploit their slaves.

Antebellum slavery was a profitable institution and one that encouraged masters to treat their slaves more like animals than human beings. Although slave prices fluctuated on an annual basis, young males between the ages of 18 and 30 sold for $500 to $700 in the Upper South during the 1820s. A healthy female slave, in her childbearing years, was worth almost twice as much. Eager to enhance their profits, some owners began to breed slaves for the Deep South market. One of these was Edward Covey, who bought a slave named Caroline because she was said to be a breeder. Covey rented a male slave from a neighbor and tied him to Caroline each night. By the end of the year, Caroline gave birth to twins, who were subsequently sold in order to increase Covey's landholdings on the Eastern Shore.[18] However, a rebellious slave was a bad investment because such a slave could stir up trouble among other slaves, which might lead to limited productivity, escapes, or worse, an insurrection. Potential buyers were able to determine the personal disposition of unruly slaves by examining their bodies for signs of physical abuse. Male slaves who toiled in the fields could expect to be lashed with a leather whip. Enslaved women experienced sexual exploitation at the hands of owners and overseers. Often slave women were forced into cohabitation and pregnancy by their masters. If they were unwilling, they, too, were beaten. Those slaves who tried to escape were often forced to wear bells on their arms, neck, or head. Some were even muzzled. Masters occasionally branded their slaves like cattle to show proof of their ownership.[19]

Such inhumane treatment, designed to produce humility and submission in the slave as well as to extract more work, inspired revenge among some slaves. Poisoning was one method. If arsenic or other similar compounds were unavailable, slaves resorted to mixing ground glass in the gravy for their masters' table. Several slaves were convicted for murdering their masters and overseers in this way.[20] Another common method of resistance was circumventing the master's control. Slaves lessened their productivity by conducting general work slowdowns and feigning illness. Some broke tools or sabotaged equipment and blamed it on clumsiness.[21] Still others, who were more desperate, deprived the master of their labor by practicing self-mutilation and even committing suicide. Slaves cut off their toes, fingers, and hands in order to render themselves ineffective as field workers. Suicide was rare and usually occurred en route to or upon arrival in the United States from Africa, or when a slave mother took her own life and those of her children to prevent them from being sold to the Deep South.[22]

The most sensational form of resistance was the conspiracy to revolt. While slaveholders considered the revolt a sinister and barbaric act committed by those who were ungrateful for the benevolence they had been shown, the slaves accepted the revolt as the price of freedom. Revolts, or conspiracies to revolt, persisted to 1865. Perhaps the most famous one was the 1831 insurrection of Nat Turner. a slave from Southampton County, Virginia. Turner was a self-styled preacher who had run away and then decided to return to his master. Interpreting a solar eclipse as a sign, Turner, in February 1831, decided that the time had come to lead his fellow slaves out of bondage. On August 21, Turner began the revolt by murdering his master, Joseph Travis, and his family. He then led a group of fellow slaves through the Virginia countryside, brutally murdering some 60 white slaveholders and their families. Turner had planned to raise an army of slaves and lead an insurrection against white planters. The white backlash was overwhelming and harsh. Militiamen not only attacked Turner and his lieutenants, but also other slaves not involved in the plot. Captured on October 30, Turner was hanged less than two weeks later and more than 200 slaves were indiscriminately killed in retaliation for the conspiracy. The revolt not only caused Southerners to pass further laws restricting black freedoms, but also inspired a sterner defense of slavery by Southern writers, including Thomas R. Dew and George Fitzhugh. Citing biblical references to slavery, these writers argued that the institution was sanctioned by God and beneficial to both races because blacks were not equipped to care for themselves and needed white, paternalistic masters to protect them.[23]

Inhumane treatment, the prospect of sale to the Deep South, and the proslavery mindset of white Southerners were all factors that influenced a slave's decision to run away. Other reasons included the death of a master, which caused great fear and apprehension among slaves about their own future as well as the future of their families; escaping the sexual advances of white masters; and, above all, the desire to be reunited with family members.[24]

The idea of escaping bondage was a constant temptation for Minty, who would later recall that she "grew up neglected like a weed." Though Edward Brodess was "never unnecessarily cruel" to her, he often hired her out to others who "proved to be tyrannical and brutal."[25] For example, Minty, at age five, was hired out as a nursemaid to a woman by the name of Miss Susan, who had an "awful temper and stormed around the house calling her all kinds of names." But she was given no instruction on how to care for the infant. "That baby was always in my lap except when it was asleep, or its mother was feeding it," she said. There were occasions when Minty was forced to sit up all night to rock the baby as her mistress "lay upon her bed with a whip under her pillow, and slept." If the baby cried for any reason, Miss Susan whipped Minty across the face and neck, believing that she was incapable of doing anything unless she was beaten.[26]

On another occasion, Miss Susan threatened Minty for stealing a lump of sugar. "One morning, after breakfast, Miss Susan had the baby, and I stood by the table waiting to take it. Near me was a bowl of lumps of white sugar. That sugar right by me looked so good and my mistress's back was turned so I put my fingers in the bowl to take one lump. She turned and saw me, and I just flew out the door. I run, and run, and run. I passed many a house, but I didn't dare to stop, for they all knew my Missus and they would send me back."[27] Hoping to escape another lash-ing, Minty hid in a neighbor's pigsty for five days until she was so hungry she returned to the house, where she received a violent beating.[28] She eventually learned to protect herself from such abuse by wrapping herself in additional layers of clothing, and crying out as if she felt the pain whenever she was whipped.[29]

Minty, at age six, was hired out to a planter by the name of James Cook. "I used to sleep on the floor in front of the fireplace," she recalled. "I used to think all the time, 'If I could only get home and get in my mother's bed.' And the funny part of that was my mother never had a bed in her life. Nothing but a board box nailed up against the wall and straw laid on it."[30] Still, she yearned to be with her mother and often spoke of her childhood homesickness. Mrs. Cook attempted to teach Minty the trade of weaving, a skill that might have allowed her to live at home with her mother. But Minty hated her mistress and refused to learn. Instead, she was sent into nearby marshes to check her master's muskrat traps. Even after she contracted the measles, the youngster was ordered into waist-high cold water to check the traps. She became gravely ill and was sent back to her mother, who nursed her back to health. Desperate to protect her daughter, Rit persuaded Brodess to keep her away from the Cooks. Although Brodess agreed, Minty was hired out elsewhere.[31]

As she grew older and stronger, the young slave girl was assigned grueling field work. She chopped wood, hauled timber, pulled barges, and plowed fields. The work allowed her to develop the great physical strength and endurance for which she would later be known. She also learned the healing power of plants and herbs from the swamps and marshlands of Dorchester County. This knowledge would later prove beneficial in aiding runaways who were injured on the secret journey to freedom.[32]

Most of the money Minty earned was given to Edward Brodess, though he did allow her to keep some for herself. On one occasion, she earned and saved enough money to purchase a pair of steers to assist her in the fields. On her many errands to the local stables and dry-goods store, she must have been tempted to buy other animals or tools that would lessen the burden of the hard labor.

Sometime in 1834, the adolescent Minty was sent to a dry-goods store for some supplies. There, she encountered another slave who had left the fields without permission. When his overseer arrived to take him back, the slave resisted him. Furious, the overseer demanded that Minty help restrain the young man. She refused. As the slave broke free, the overseer grabbed a two-pound weight from the store counter and threw it at him. He missed and struck Minty instead. She later contended that the weight "broke my skull" and might have killed her had it not been for her thick hair, which "had never been combed and stood out like a bushel basket."

Bleeding and unconscious, Minty was returned to the Brodess house, where she remained without medical care for two days. She would slip into a lethargic sleep from which it was almost impossible to awaken. The spells would come without warning. Often the sleep was interrupted by nightmares. Despite her illness, Minty was hired out again. She toiled in the fields "with blood and sweat rolling down [her] face until [she] couldn't see."[33] When the farmer returned her to Brodess he told him that Minty was "not worth a sixpence." No longer a strong young woman, she was now unable to do the grueling labor that had been expected of her, and Brodess tried, unsuccessfully, to sell her.[34]

As a result of the head injury, Minty began having severe headaches and seizures. Often these episodes would leave her in a trance-like state, though she claimed to be aware of her surroundings. Because the episodes occurred so suddenly and without warning, they alarmed her family, who were unable to wake her until the incident passed. Tubman's biographers are divided on the reasons for this behavior. Some believe that she suffered from temporal lobe epilepsy (TLE) as a result of the head injury. Seizures, sleeping spells, and visions followed by episodes of tremendous anxiety and crippling fatigue are typical of TLE. In addition, TLE visions often assume the form of spiritual or religious hallucinations, something Tubman experienced for the rest of her life.[35] Other historians believe that the injury triggered the onset of psychic abilities that allowed Minty to experience out-of-body travel, psychic visions and clairvoyance, and clairaudience, through which she heard the voice of God. She claimed that God "spoke directly to my soul" during these trance-like states, and guided her through all of her dangerous journeys. In addition, contemporaries noted that Tubman had a strange power over all animals—another indication of psychic ability—and insisted that she never feared the bloodhounds who dogged her trail when she became an Underground Railroad agent.[36] Whatever the reason, Minty's head injury occurred at a point in her life when she was becoming deeply religious.

Slaves used religion both as a means of defiance and a source of hope. While many were exposed to the conventional religious beliefs and practices of their masters, their instruction was circumscribed. White ministers and owners emphasized Old Testament teachings that encouraged slavery and obedience to one's master. The lessons stressed that slaves did not deserve freedom, that it was God's will that they were enslaved, and that the devil created a desire for liberty in those who ran away. Few slaves were deluded by such teachings. Instead, they formulated new religious ideas and practices in the slave quarters. These were grounded in Old Testament passages that emphasized the struggle of Jews in bondage and their deliverance from slavery as well as an adaptation of African folk beliefs and practices. Praise meetings that would begin on a Saturday or Sunday evening and last far into the night were characterized by enthusiastic shouting, the singing of spirituals in a call-and-response pattern, and highly emotional preaching. Often the sermons stressed the point that the master might be able to inflict pain on a slave's body, but he could not harm his soul. Such religious services allowed the slave to shift his attention from the physical and psychological brutality of his immediate condition to a brighter future awaiting him in an afterlife. It also allowed slaves to develop a strong sense of group solidarity in order to protect themselves from the most oppressive features of slavery.[37] White masters were intimidated by these gatherings. Many of the owners believed that the prayer meetings of their slaves fostered plans for conspiracy and rebellion. As a result, invitations to attend white churches bordered on compulsion.[38]

As a child, Minty had been told Bible stories by her mother, and she was occasionally forced to attend the services held by Dr. Anthony Thompson, Jr., who was a licensed Methodist minister. But Minty and her parents might also have been influenced by Episcopal, Baptist, and Catholic teachings since the Pattisons, Thompsons, and Brodesses initially belonged to Anglican and Episcopal churches in Dorchester County before they became Methodists. In addition, some of the white Tubmans and Rosses were originally Catholic. Accordingly, Minty's religious beliefs might have been a composite of several different Christian traditions that were adapted to the evangelical emphasis on spiritual freedom. Like many slaves, she rejected white interpretations of scripture that encouraged slavery. Instead she found guidance in the Old Testament stories of deliverance.[39] The evangelical emphasis on spiritual freedom was part of the core theology of many black denominations that were formed within the Methodist tradition in the early 19th century, such as the African Methodist Episcopal Church. Oral tradition suggests that Minty, her parents, and many of Bucktown's free and enslaved blacks attended Bazzel's Methodist Episcopal Church, just a half mile southeast of the Brodess property, and Scott's Chapel, another black Methodist church.[40]

Regardless of her place of worship or the specific denominational influence, Minty's faith was a strong and abiding influence in her life. She claimed to hear the voice of God and she "prayed all the time." "I was always talking to the Lord," she later told her biographer Sarah Bradford. "When I went to the horse trough to wash my face, and took up the water in my hands, I said, 'Oh Lord, wash me, make me clean.' When I took up the towel to wipe my face and hands, I cried, 'Oh Lord, for Jesus' sake, wipe away all my sins!'"[41] One of her prayers was answered in 1840 when her father, Ben Ross, became a free man.

When Ben's owner, Anthony Thompson, Sr., died in November 1836, he provided for the slave's manumission in his will. Though he was now his own man, Ben, age 55, decided to remain near his family on the Eastern Shore and work as a timber estimator and foreman for Thompson's son, Dr. Anthony Thompson, Jr., who owned a large plantation called Popular Neck in neighboring Caroline County. Ben was also employed by a local shipbuilder, James A. Stewart, who owned extensive property and timberland throughout the region.[42]

Minty, now age 18, was so proud of her father that she decided to abandon her slave name. To honor her parents, she would be known as "Harriet Ross."

NOTES

1. See William J. Switala, *Underground Railroad in Delaware, Maryland, and West Virginia* (Mechanicsburg, PA: Stackpole Books, 2004), 61–62.

2. Clara Small, "Abolitionists, Free Blacks, and Runaway Slaves: Surviving Slavery on Maryland's Eastern Shore," in A History of African Americans of Delaware and Maryland's Eastern Shore, ed. Carole C. Marks (Wilmington, DE: Christian Council of Delaware and Maryland's Eastern Shore and the University of Delaware's Black American Studies Department, 1996), 55–57; and Switala, Underground Railroad, 64–70.

3. Her recent biographers speculate on the year of Tubman's birth. Though she claimed that she was born in 1825, her death certificate records 1815 as the year of her birth. As a result, Catherine Clinton contends that Tubman's birth date was 1820, the same date recorded on her gravestone; see Catherine Clinton, Harriet Tubman: The Road to Freedom (New York: Little, Brown, 2004), 4. Kate Larson, on the other hand, argues that 1822 was the year of Tubman's birth, based on a midwife payment and several other historical documents; see Kate Clifford Larson, Bound for the Promised Land: Harriet Tubman, Portrait of an American Hero (New York: Ballantine Books, 2004), 16. Jean Humez offers a compromise between these two positions, writing that "the best current evidence suggests that Tubman was born in 1820, but it might have been a year or two later"; see Jean Humez, Harriet Tubman: The Life and the Life Stories (Madison: University of Wisconsin, 2003), 12.

4. Larson, Bound for the Promised Land, 10–11, 16; Humez, Life and Life Stories, 12.

5. Larson, Bound for the Promised Land, 10, 16; Humez, Life and Life Stories, 355.

6. Letter of Calvin Mowbray to James McGowan, Cambridge, Maryland: July 12, 1984.

7. Humez, Life and Life Stories, 355, note 9. Humez adds that Rit took the name Harriet Ross and was known by that name for the remainder of her life.

8. Larson, Bound for the Promised Land, 311–312. The nine children of Ben Ross and Harriet Green were: Linah (born in 1808); Mariah Ritty (1811); Soph (1813); Robert (1816); Minty (1820); Ben (1823); Rachel (1825); Henry (1830): and Moses (1832).

9. Larson, Bound for the Promised Land, 15.

10. Larson, Bound for the Promised Land, 16–17.

11. Peter Kolchin, *American Slavery, 1619–1877* (New York: Hill & Wang, 1993), 100–102.

12. Sarah H. Bradford, *Harriet Tubman: The Moses of Her People* (1886; reprint, Secaucus, NJ: Citadel Press, 1961), 15; Larson, *Bound for the Promised Land*, 29; Humez, *Life and Life Stories*, 12–14; and Clinton, *Road to Freedom*, 10.

13. Interview of Harriet Tubman, quoted in Benjamin Drew, *The Refugee: A North-Side View of Slavery* (1855; reprint, ed. Tilden G. Edelstein [Reading MA: Addison-Wesley Publishing Company, 1969]), 20.

14. Clinton, *Road to Freedom*, 13; Larson, *Bound for the Promised Land*, 33–34.

15. Interview of Ben Ross (a.k.a. James Seward) quoted in Drew, *The Refugee*, 27.

16. Interview of Robert Ross (a.k.a., John Seward) in Drew, *The Refugee*, 27.

17. Larson, *Bound for the Promised Land*, 37.

18. James Oliver Horton and Lois E. Horton, *Slavery and the Making of America* (New York: Oxford University Press, 2005), 98–99.

19. See Kenneth M. Stampp, *The Peculiar Institution: Slavery in the Antebellum South* (New York: Viking, 1956), 4–6; Eugene Genovese, *Roll Jordan, Roll: The World the Slaveholders Made* (New York: Pantheon, 1974); and Horton, *Slavery and the Making of America*, 47–84.

20. John Hope Franklin, *From Slavery to Freedom: A History of Negro Americans*, 5th ed. (New York: Knopf, 1980), 152.

21. Horton, *Slavery and the Making of America*, 120.

22. Horton, *Slavery and the Making of America*, 130–131; and Franklin, *From Slavery to Freedom*, 150–151.

23. Horton, *Slavery and the Making of America*, 112–116, 143; and Franklin, *From Slavery to Freedom*, 155.

24. John Hope Franklin and Loren Schweninger, *Runaway Slaves: Rebels on the Plantation* (New York: Oxford University Press, 1999), 7–48.

25. Harriet Tubman, quoted in Sarah H. Bradford, *Scenes in the Life of Harriet Tubman* (Auburn, NY: W. J. Moses, 1869), 9.

26. Clinton, *Road to Freedom*, 17–18; Larson, *Bound for the Promised Land*, 39.

27. Bradford, *Moses of Her People*, 135–136.

28. Larson, *Bound for the Promised Land*, 40.

29. Clinton, *Road to Freedom*, 19.

30. Harriet Tubman, quoted in Emma P. Telford, "Harriet: The Modern Moses of Heroism and Visions" (Cayuga County Museum, Auburn, New York, ca. 1905), 4; and Bradford, *Scenes in the Life of Harriet Tubman*, 12.

31. Larson, *Bound for the Promised Land*, 38.

32. Bradford, *Moses of Her People*, 9–10; and Larson, *Bound for the Promised Land*, 56.

33. Harriet Tubman, quoted in Telford, "Modern Moses of Heroism and Visions," 5; And Bradford, *Scenes in the Life of Harriet Tubman*, 74.

34. Clinton, *Road to Freedom*, 22.

35. Larson, *Bound for the Promised Land*, 42–43.

36. James A. McGowan, "The Psychic Life of Harriet Tubman," *Visions Magazine* (March 1995): 1–3. McGowan claims that the onset of Tubman's psychic life parallels that of other well-known, contemporary psychics like Peter Hurkos, the Dutch psychometrist. Parapsychological records are replete with similar cases in which individuals began experiencing and manifesting psychic awareness after head injuries. Some cases occur after being struck by lightning, others after undergoing prolonged periods of intense fever.

37. John W. Blassingame, *The Slave Community: Plantation Life in the Antebellum South* (New York: Oxford University, 1978, paperback edition), 60–66, 75–76.

38. Franklin, *From Slavery to Freedom*, 144.

39. Clinton, *Road to Freedom*, 20.

40. Larson, *Bound for the Promised Land*, 45–47.

41. Harriet Tubman, quoted in Bradford, *Scenes in the Life of Harriet Tubman*, 14.

42. Larson, *Bound for the Promised Land*, 97–98; and Clinton, *Road to Freedom*, 23–24.

Chapter 2

LIBERTY OR DEATH,
1841–1850

Harriet's growing sense of independence coincided with a steady de-cline in Maryland's slave labor. Changing economic conditions placed a higher premium on more mobile, free labor on the Eastern Shore. In Dorchester County, the slave population dropped by 20 percent, to just over 4,000 between 1790 and 1850, and the free black population exploded from just 528 to almost 4,000 during the same period. Har-riet, now in her mid-20s, capitalized on the situation by negotiating a work-for-hire arrangement with Brodess. Under the agreement, she was permitted to rent out her labor as long as she paid him a set annual fee of 50 or 60 dollars. The arrangement allowed her to work for her father, now a free man who supervised the cutting and hauling of lumber for the Baltimore shipyards.[1] She also met and married a free black man named John Tubman sometime around 1844.[2]

Tubman, age 26 at the time of the marriage, was of "dark mulatto complexion" and stood 5 feet, 9½ inches tall. He was born and raised in Parson's Creek, Dorchester County.[3] Not much more is known about him, or how the couple met, or the circumstances surrounding their engagement.[4] What is certain was that marriage between a slave and a free black was not recognized by law. Instead, the union was based on a commitment the couple made to each other and with the permission of the slave owner, who had the legal right to dissolve the marriage in the future.[5] If there was a wedding ceremony, it probably took place on a Sunday, the slaves' only day off from work. Preachers sometimes conducted the ceremony, but most couples participated in an African custom called "jumping the broom." The bride and groom would each jump backward over a broom handle held a few inches above the floor. This was done in the presence of witnesses who acknowledged that they had become husband and wife.[6] Afterwards, Harriet left her mother's quarters on the Brodess farm and presumably lived with Tubman near the Peters Neck area. She also took his surname, which she kept for the rest of her life.[7]

While such mixed marriages between a free black and a slave were common on Maryland's Eastern Shore, the Tubman union presented difficulties related to social as well as legal status. Harriet's skin complexion was unmistakably black and reflected her Ashanti heritage. Several contemporaries referred to her skin complexion as "coal black," "jet black," and "not a drop of white blood in her veins."[8] Harriet's black skin complexion made her, according to antebellum society's social conventions, inferior to her husband John, who was a mulatto. This distinction in social status evolved over time, but by the 1840s was recognized by the federal government as a means of legal identification.

Historically, the term *black* was used in the United States to refer to "any person with any known African black ancestry" and reflected the "long experience with slavery." *Mulatto*, on the other hand, was originally used to identify the offspring of a "pure African Negro" and a "pure white" person. In the antebellum South, however, whites blurred the distinction by adopting the one-drop rule, meaning that a single drop of black blood made a person black.[9] This revision was made as miscegenation increased between owners and their female slaves and was done in order to increase the human chattel of the master as well as to maximize his financial income, which was based on slave labor. The definitions of *black* and *mulatto* also appear to have been established by the federal government. United States Census takers, for example, were extremely careful to distinguish between the following terms:

Blacks: "Those having three-fourths or more of African blood."

Mulattos: "Those having three-eighths to five eighths African blood."

Quadroons: "Those having one-fourth African blood."

Octoroons: "Those having one-eighth or any trace of African blood."[10]

In addition, there existed a similar caste system based on skin color among antebellum blacks. Though whiteness was denied to anyone with African blood, those African Americans with lighter skin commanded a higher position in the slave community as well as in the free black community. Blacks with biracial ancestry justified their social status by reversing the federal government's definitions and citing the amount of *white* blood they possessed. An octoroon had seven-eighths or more white blood, a quadroon three-fourths white blood, and a mulatto five eighths to three-eighths white blood. Accordingly, an octoroon believed himself to be superior to a quadroon; a quadroon felt superior to a mulatto; and a mulatto felt superior to all who were less than mulattos, though all mixed bloods were called mulattos.[11]

This caste system was so entrenched in the slave community that there were slave women in the Deep South who did not resist the sexual advances of their white masters because of "the prestige that such a relationship would bring for them" and the "social acceptability" their mulatto offspring would gain. In fact, miscegenation was so common in the antebellum South that by 1850, there were 246,000 mulatto slaves out of a total slave population of 3.2 million. Ten years later, in 1860, there were a total of 411,000 mulatto slaves out of a total slave population of 3.9 million.[12] Thus, the caste system that emerged from the distinctions between black and mulatto was accepted—if not celebrated—by both African Americans and whites in antebellum society.

The racial distinction must have also contributed to Harriet's low self-esteem as a youngster and reinforced the already subordinate legal status women held in relation to their husbands in antebellum society. In addition, since Harriet was a slave, any children born to her and John would also be enslaved. John must have loved Harriet dearly if he forfeited his legal and parental rights to the children they might conceive. Perhaps the couple was planning to purchase Harriet's freedom from Brodess to avoid that situation.[13] In fact, the year after the marriage, Harriet attempted to obtain her freedom through the courts. Rit had told her daughter that Atthow Pattison, her first owner, had provided for the manumission of all her children in his last will and testament, but that Edward Brodess had reneged on the promise. Determined to find the will, Harriet hired a lawyer who consulted the Dorchester County Court Records and found it. But Brodess pressed his own claim, preventing any legal action on her part. Together with Brodess's refusal to grant Harriet her freedom, the Pattison claim provided even greater motivation for her to flee from bondage.[14]

Brodess continued to struggle at farming. His Bucktown property was too small to produce a profitable return. Lacking the resources to expand his holdings, he turned to selling his slaves for cash. In the early 1840s, Brodess illegally sold Harriet's older sisters, Linah and Soph, who were supposed to be freed at age 45. Linah was separated from her two children, Kessiah and Harriet, in the sale.[15] Brodess also made an effort to sell Harriet, even after she was married, but she prayed that God would "change his heart" until March of 1849 when she learned that he "planned to send her to the Deep South."[16] Initially devastated by the news, Harriet's sorrow quickly turned to rage and she began praying for vindication. "Lord," she asked, "if you ain't never going to change that man's heart, kill him and take him out of the way so he won't do no more mischief."[17] She received her wish on March 7, 1849, when Brodess died unexpectedly at the age of 47.[18] Guilt-stricken, Harriet later confessed that she would "give the world full of silver and gold to bring his poor soul back."[19] It was a fascinating change of heart.

Was Harriet hoping for her own redemption, or Brodess's resurrection? After experiencing the sale of family members and her own exploitation at his hands, she certainly wouldn't want Brodess to return. He would have only increased her misery by selling her off. It is more plausible that Harriet feared the wrath of God for wishing death on another human being, even as wicked as Brodess had been to her. Her guilt was more reflective of a desire to be faithful to God and His will, and not yield to a sinful desire for revenge.

Ironically, Brodess's death increased the likelihood of Harriet being sold. His widow, Eliza, needed to pay off her deceased husband's many debts and planned to sell the family's remaining slaves. Harriet took matters into her own hands, in spite of her husband's pleas that she remain with him on the Eastern Shore.[20] "There was one of two things I had a right to—liberty or death," she explained later. "If I could not have one, I would have the other."[21]

On September 17, 1849, Harriet and her two brothers, Ben and Henry, escaped from slavery. Since the three siblings had been hired out to work on the same plantation, Eliza Brodess probably did not realize that they had run away.[22] Not until two weeks later did she post an advertisement for their capture in the *Cambridge Democrat*, offering a reward of up to $100 for each one:

> Ran away from the subscriber on Monday the 17th of September, three negroes, named as follows: HARRY [Henry], age about 19 years, has on one side of his neck a welt, just under the ear, he is of a dark chestnut color, about 5 feet 8 or nine inches high; BEN, age about 25 years, is very quick to speak when spoken to, he is of chestnut color, about six feet high; MINTY, age about 27 years, is of a chestnut color, fine looking, and about 5 feet high. One hundred dollars reward will be given for each of the above named negroes, if taken out of the state, and $50 each if taken in the State. They must be lodged in Baltimore, Easton or Cambridge Jail, in Maryland.
>
> —Eliza Ann Brodess
> Near Bucktown, Dorchester county, Md.
> October 3, 1849[23]

Once they set out for the North, however, Harriet and her brothers quickly scuttled their mission. Though they had set their sights on Pennsylvania, realizing that it was a free state, none of the group knew how to get there. They constantly argued over directions and feared for their safety, knowing that if caught they faced almost certain sale to the Deep South. In addition, Ben, who had recently become a father, began to entertain second thoughts. When the brothers decided to return to the Eastern Shore, they forced Harriet to come with them, and she reluctantly agreed.[24] Questions remain as to why Harriet agreed to return to bondage. It was an uncharacteristic decision, considering the rebellious spirit that would later become part of her international reputation. In addition, she was at least four years older than Ben and a full decade older than Henry. Harriet had also helped her mother to raise the two boys. Shouldn't they have deferred to their elder sister's authority and continued on their journey to freedom?

It is important to note that family was the most important priority in Tubman's life. Although she was leaving her own husband, Harriet considered it a temporary separation. She planned to return for him once she established a new life in the North. At the same time, she understood what must have been a tremendous emotional and psychological desire for Ben to return to his wife and newborn baby. Harriet would not allow herself to stand in the way of the reunion. Why then didn't she continue the journey northward on her own? Perhaps she was hesitant because of her unfamiliarity with the geography and her own abilities to survive in a border region that was quickly becoming a battleground between proslavery and antislavery elements. She was right to be concerned.

Prior to 1850, most runaway slaves were single men between the ages of 18 and 32. Not only did they have the physical strength and stamina to evade capture and survive the challenges of a treacherous and unknown journey, but they had no family commitments tying them to the plantation. Female escapes were much less common, and when they did occur, women almost always traveled in groups accompanied by male fugitives.[25] For a woman to attempt an escape alone was either extremely brave or foolhardy. She had a much better chance of being caught than making a successful journey to freedom. Harriet realized these things. She had ample opportunity to run away, having been hired out by Brodess as an adolescent and as a young adult. Yet she never took advantage of the opportunity to escape until 1849. Once she made the aborted attempt, though, it was difficult for her return to return to slavery.

Haunted by prophetic visions, Harriet saw horsemen coming for her and heard the terrifying screams of women and children. She traveled with these apocalyptic horsemen over fields, towns, rivers, and mountains until they reached a great fence. Fearing that she did not have the power to fly over, Harriet felt herself losing strength and sinking rapidly into a widening abyss. Then suddenly she was rescued by ladies dressed in white who pulled her across the threshold into freedom. Night after night Harriet experienced the dream. Her only relief came through incessant prayer.[26] Finally, in late October, Harriet struck out on her own. Realizing that it would be too dangerous to reveal her intentions to her family, she sang a farewell song which, like many of the Negro spirituals, bore a double meaning:

When that old chariot comes,
I'm going to leave you,
I'm bound for the promised land,
Friends, I'm going to leave you.
I'm sorry, friends, to leave you,
Farewell! Oh, farewell!
But I'll meet you in the morning,
When you reach the promised land;
On the other side of Jordan,
For I'm bound for the promised land.[27]

Since Harriet was unfamiliar with the upper part of the Delmarva Peninsula, she resorted to the same practice of the many runaways who had preceded her: she traveled at night, following the North Star, "feeling her way, finding out who were [her] friends."[28] During the day, she hid, taking refuge in the woods or marshlands. At some point on the 100-mile journey, Harriet crossed the Chesapeake and Delaware Canal, where free black dock workers willingly provided her with food and shelter and guided her through hidden tunnels and pathways along the marshy creeks and sodden woodlands of eastern Maryland. Impelled by visions of a pillar of clouds during the day and following the North Star by night, Harriet benefited from the aid of a white woman, Hannah Leverton, the wife of a Quaker mill owner. Handing the fugitive a slip of paper with two names on it, Leverton concealed Harriet in a wagon and had her husband drive her to the Delaware border. Since Harriet was illiterate, the slip of paper was probably intended for the next station master—that is, the next stop on the Underground Railroad—and served as confirmation that she was indeed a fugitive. After reaching the border, Leverton's husband directed Harriet to the house of the agent whose name was listed on the paper. She still had 80 miles to go before reaching Wilmington, the home of Thomas Garrett, a Quaker abolitionist whose Underground Railroad station was the last stop in Delaware before the Pennsylvania boundary dividing the free and slave states. Somehow Harriet managed to navigate her way around Dover and Smyrna, towns that were hospitable to slave catchers and professional bounty hunters hired by owners to capture their runaway property. When she arrived at Wilmington, Garrett contacted another agent, who guided Tubman across the Mason-Dixon Line and into the free state of Pennsylvania.[29]

Although Tubman left few details about her journey, some of her biographers speculate that Garrett sent her on to Philadelphia by way of Chester County, Pennsylvania.[30] Located just north of the Mason-Dixon Line, Chester County was revered by fugitives as the gateway to the Promised Land. The region was blessed with a series of parallel hills whose thickly wooded slopes offered a natural avenue of escape as well as effective concealment for runaways. Routes for the Underground Railroad came through both Delaware and Maryland. A northern route entered Lancaster County from Maryland by way of Fulton, then to the north through East Drumore, Paradise, and Salisbury, led next into Chester County by way of Honeybrook, continued through to Phoenixville, then to Norristown, and finally to Philadelphia. Another major route cut through the center of Chester County, extending from Wilmington into Kennett, East Marlborough, Newlin, Downingtown, Lionville, Kimberton, and Phoenixville. Still another major route headed in an easterly direction, beginning at Wilmington and extending through Kennett, East Bradford, West Chester, Willistown, and then to Philadelphia. Thomas Garrett, whose Wilmington home was the starting point for two of the three major routes, maintained an extensive network of agents throughout the Chester County. Some were family members, others were friends, and most were Quaker abolitionists.

The nerve center of Garrett's Chester County operation was located at Kennett, just a few short miles over the Mason-Dixon Line. Kennett was the home of Garrett's in-laws, Isaac and Dinah Mendenhall, as well as two other Quaker couples, John and Hannah Cox and Allen and Maria Agnew. Like Garrett, all three of these couples were dedicated Underground Railroad agents who opened their homes to fugitives. Thus, when a fugitive reached Kennett, the particular route he took depended largely on circumstance. Since Kennett was like the hub of a wagon wheel with spokes leading in all directions, runaways had several secondary routes open to them. Roads led east to Philadelphia and New Jersey; north to West Chester, Downingtown, Phoenixville, Lionville, and Kimberton; northwest to Ercildoun and Coatesville; west to Avondale, West Grove, and into Lancaster County. To the south were the villages of New Garden, Landenberg, and Hockessin, Delaware. Consequently, if there were no space available at one station, a fugitive's route could easily be altered to accommodate the problem. Alternative stations were often used when a fugitive was being pursued, if only to avoid predictability. In most cases, the destination was Philadelphia, where a sizeable free black population offered camouflage for runaways. In the future, Harriet, as a conductor, would become very familiar with Chester County's Underground Railroad network and the various agents who operated it.[31] But, in 1849, she experienced the overwhelming joy of her own liberation after crossing over the Mason-Dixon line.

"When I found I had crossed that magic line separating the land of bondage from the land of freedom," Harriet recalled, "I looked at my hands to see if I was the same person. There was such a glory over everything. The sun came out through the trees, and over the fields, and I felt like I was in Heaven."[32] Harriet's elation was short-lived, though. She soon realized that "there was no one to welcome [her] to the land of freedom." "I was a stranger in a strange land," she confessed. "My home, after all, was down in Maryland; because my father, my mother, my brothers, and sisters, and friends were there." It was at that point that Harriet vowed to "make a home in the North" and, "with God's help, bring them all there."[33]

Once settled in Philadelphia, Tubman found work and made several important contacts with the Philadelphia Vigilance Committee, an interracial antislavery organization that aided fugitives. The City of Brotherly Love proved to be an ideal place to settle. Philadelphia boasted the largest free black community in the North with a population of 15,000, nearly one-third from Delaware or Maryland. Mobility and economic opportunity were also accessible to African Americans, as reflected by the city's growing black middle class. The free black community also established its own churches and charities. The most influential of these institutions was the Mother Bethel African Methodist Episcopal Church, founded in 1791 by the Reverend Richard Allen, a former slave. Patterning its discipline on Methodism, the AME Church quickly became the leading body among the city's black Methodists with over 4,000 members by 1820. The church not only performed the usual religious rituals and guarded the moral discipline of the community, but also provided and promoted education, fraternal societies, and recreation for its members. By the late 1850s, Mother Bethel was one of nearly 20 African American churches in the city. Whether they were AME, Baptist, or Methodist, the churches offered their congregations an open forum to discuss the need for expanding liberties, to challenge slavery, and even to plan assistance for runaways.[34] For Harriet, Philadelphia marked a dramatic change from the life she led on Maryland's Eastern Shore. But she acclimated to her new life quickly, making the transformation from a bondswoman to a free black woman with relative ease. She longed to have her family with her, to have them enjoy the same opportunities that freedom had afforded her. Within a year's time, Harriet began making plans to return to the Eastern Shore to guide other family members to the North.[35]

Tubman was just one of a steady flow of slaves who ran away from the Eastern Shore between 1847 and 1849. Frustrated slaveholders suspected a conspiracy of abolitionists tempting slaves to escape, and voiced their concern in the August 14, 1849, issue of the *Easton Star:*

> RUNAWAYS. Almost every week we hear of one or more slaves making their escape and if something is not speedily done to put a stop to it, that kind of property will hardly be worth owning. There seems to be some system about this business, and we strongly suspect they are assisted in their escape by an organized band of abolitionists. We think it advisable for the Slave Holders of the Eastern Shore to establish a line of Telegraph down the peninsula, and organize an efficient police force along the line, as the most effectual means of protecting their slave property, and recovering such as may attempt to make their escape. At present, all efforts to recover them after they once made their escape appears fruitless.[36]

To be sure, Harriet's escape from slavery in 1849 was timely, for there were forces already in motion that would lead the nation into a civil war. The United States was rapidly expanding during the first half of the 19th century. With the purchase of the Louisiana territory from France in 1803, the federal government acquired some 828,000 square miles, almost doubling the geographical size of the country. In time, 13 new states would be carved out of the new territory, and the admission of the earliest of these would stir bitter debates in Congress over the expansion of slavery. The first test case came in 1819 when Missouri applied for statehood. Missouri was located along the same latitude as several free states. Its entry into the Union as a slave state would have moved slavery northward and upset the congressional balance of 11 slave states and 11 free states. While Northerners intended to limit slavery to the South, Southerners sought to expand cotton production, which required slave labor, into the new states. Heated, sometimes vicious, debates broke out on the floor of Congress until Senator Henry Clay of Kentucky brokered a compromise. Missouri would gain admission as a slave state if Maine could enter as a free state. In addition, Clay established a line at the latitude of 36° 30'. Territories north of that line would remain free, and those to the south could maintain slavery. The so-called Missouri Compromise was passed by Congress in 1820, and determined the extension of slavery for the next 30 years.[37]

Sectional conflict surfaced again in 1850 when Congress became consumed with the issue of whether extensive territories acquired after the Mexican War should prohibit slavery. Southern Democrats who favored the expansion of slavery squared off against northern Whigs who feared that if slavery were permitted in the West, then wealthy plantation owners would buy up all the land, leaving little for less affluent farmers. In addition, many northern Democrats believed that new plantations meant that the western territories would be populated with blacks and they had no desire to live among a large African American population. Ironically, the white supremacist beliefs of the Democratic Party led to radically different conclusions, splintering it into southern and northern branches. In 1846, the rift intensified when Pennsylvania congressman David Wilmot, one of the alienated Northern Democrats, proposed that slavery be prohibited from any of the new territories that the United States might acquire from Mexico. Though the Wilmot Proviso passed in the House of Representatives several times, it was repeatedly rejected by the Senate, where Southerners enjoyed the edge.

But each round of voting heightened sectional tensions and led disaf-
fected Northern Democrats to launch a Free Soil Party, which focused
not on ending slavery where it already existed but on preventing it in the
new Western territories of California, Texas, Oregon, Washington, and
New Mexico.[38]

When California applied for statehood in 1850, the hostilities
reached a climax. President Zachary Taylor tried to settle the crisis by
granting immediate statehood to California and New Mexico without
specifying whether they would be free or slave states. But Southern
members of Congress blocked the action, fearing that it would set a dangerous precedent that could lead to the eventual abolition of slavery.
Again, Henry Clay, author of the 1820 Missouri Compromise, resolved
the problem by forwarding a five-part proposal: (1) California would be
admitted to the Union as a free state; (2) the remaining land won from
Mexico would be organized into two new territories—New Mexico and
Utah—and would remain open to slavery until they became states, at
which time the state legislatures could vote on the issue; (3) Texas,
whose borders had not been clearly defined since the war with Mexico,
would be prohibited from further influencing New Mexico where it had
hoped to extend slavery and, in return, receive $10 million in compen-
sation; (4) to appease antislavery Northerners, slave auctions (but not
slavery itself) would be banned in the nation's capitol, Washington, D.C.;
and (5) to mollify proslavery Southerners, the federal government would
create and enforce a new, more rigorous Fugitive Slave Law.[39]

Of all the measures, the Fugitive Slave Law was the most controversial. The law dramatically increased the power of slave owners to
capture runaway slaves. According to its provisions, a federal marshal
who did not arrest an alleged runaway was liable to a fine of $1,000.
Law-enforcement officials *everywhere* now had a duty to arrest anyone
suspected of being a runaway slave. The only evidence they needed was
the sworn testimony of the person who claimed to own that slave. In
addition, all citizens, whether they lived in the North or the South,
were required to assist in the recovery of an alleged fugitive. If a person
was caught assisting a runway, he was subject to six months' imprisonment and a $1,000 fine. Although the fugitive was entitled to a hearing
before a federal magistrate, he was not permitted to testify on his own
behalf. In other words, the Fugitive Slave Law assumed the guilt of the
accused rather than his innocence.[40]

Essentially, the Fugitive Slave Law of 1850 nullified the personal liberty laws of the New England states as well as those of New York, New Jersey, and Pennsylvania. The full force of the federal government now overrode the rights of the state in favor of the slaveholders. Not only did the law endanger fugitives, but also the welfare of free blacks who could be kidnapped and sold into bondage. Abolitionists argued in vain that the law was unconstitutional since it denied the alleged slave an impartial trial by jury and thus gave unbridled authority to slave owners to retrieve a runaway.[41] When their arguments were rejected, the abolitionists became more emboldened in their opposition and even gained the support of other white Northerners who had once been indifferent to the slavery issue.

Tubman's resolve to free the members of her family was also hastened by the passage of the infamous law. In December 1850, she received warning that her niece, Kessiah Bowley, along with Kessiah's two children—six-year-old James and baby Araminta—were to be auctioned to the highest bidder at the courthouse in Cambridge, Maryland. Kessiah's husband, John Bowley, a free black ship carpenter, had sent word to Harriet hoping to enlist her help. Horrified, she traveled to Baltimore where her brother-in-law, Tom Tubman, hid her. By means of underground messages, Bowley and Tubman devised a plan to free Kessiah and her children.

On the day of the auction at noon, a crowd of people gathered in front of the Cambridge Court House waiting for the bidding to begin. Slave auctions were among the most popular spectacles in 19th-century Maryland. People traveled from great distances to watch them just as they would a cattle show. Curiosity seekers as well as serious buyers followed the bidding. Liquor flowed just as freely as the storytelling. Kessiah and her two children stood on the courthouse steps as prospective buyers examined their bodies for any defects or bruises. It's difficult to determine just how much they knew about what was going to happen. Had John been able to reveal his plan to Kessiah? Was she prepared to flee if it failed, or to simply accept her fate? Regardless of the outcome, Kessiah realized that her life and those of her two small children would be profoundly affected by it.

Somewhere in the crowd was John Bowley. Since Maryland law did not prohibit a free black man from purchasing his family, Bowley was casting his own bids. Each time another prospective buyer challenged him, he would increase his bid, though he certainly didn't have the money on hand to cover it. The bidding was spirited and a buyer was finally secured for $600, the equivalent of about $20,000 today. John Brodess, acting for his mother, was satisfied by the sale, and Kessiah and her children were removed from the courthouse steps. When the auctioneer called for payment, however, no one came forward. The purchase had been a ruse! Bowley had made the winning bid for his wife and children and hurried them off to the nearby house of an abolitionist. At nightfall, he gathered his family and ferried them up river in a log canoe to Baltimore, 25 miles away. There they would circulate among the city's 36,000 blacks—29,000 of them free—and become indistinguishable to slave catchers and federal marshals alike. Sheltered by a family in the free black enclave of Fell's Point, Kessiah and her children were met by Harriet, who guided them safely to Philadelphia.[42]

Encouraged by her success and determined to help her family escape slavery, Tubman returned to Baltimore a few months later to bring her brother, Moses, and two other runaways to freedom.[43] These were the first of many rescues Harriet Tubman would make in her legendary career.

NOTES

1. Fergus M. Bordewich, *Bound for Canaan: The Underground Railroad and the War for the Soul of America* (New York: Amistad, 2005), 348.

2. Kate Clifford Larson, *Bound for the Promised Land: Harriet Tubman, Portrait of an American Hero* (New York: Ballantine Books, 2004), 62.

3. Calvin W. Mowbray and Maurice D. Rimpo, *Close-ups of Early Dorchester County History* (Silver Spring, MD: Family Line Publications, 1988), 58.

4. Jean Humez, *Harriet Tubman: The Life and the Life Stories* (Madison: University of Wisconsin, 2003), 15.

5. Kenneth M. Stampp, *The Peculiar Institution: Slavery in the Antebellum South* (New York: Viking, 1956), 198.

6. Alan Dundes, "'Jumping the Broom': On the Origin and Meaning of an African American Wedding Custom," *Journal of American Folklore* (1996): 324.

7. Larson, *Bound for the Promised Land*, 77, 322 n. 39.

8. See Letter, Lucy Osgood to Lydia Maria Child, June 2, 1859, Lydia Maria Child Papers, Cornell University Library, Ithaca, New York; Letter, Thomas W. Higginson to Louisa Storrow Higginson, June 17, 1859, quoted in Mary T. Higginson (ed.), *Letters and Journals of Thomas Wentworth Higginson, 1846–1906* (New York: Negro Universities Press, 1906), 81; and Franklin B. Sanborn, "Harriet Tubman," *Boston Commonwealth:* July 17, 1863.

9. F. James Davis, *Who Is Black? One Nation's Definition* (University Park, PA: Penn State Press, 1991). Defining the terms *black* and *mulatto* is complicated. Some social scientists consider the terms be descriptive of racial traits, others cultural traits, and still others ethnic traits. Sociologist F. James Davis makes some important distinctions between these categories. He defines *race* as a "category of human beings based on average differences in physical traits that are transmitted by the genes, not by blood." The term *culture*, on the other hand, is a "shared pattern of behavior and beliefs that are learned and transmitted through social communication." *Ethnicity* refers to a "group with a sense of cultural identity, such as Czech or Jewish Americans, but it may also be a racially distinctive group." Davis adds the caveat that a group that is "racially distinctive in society may be an ethnic group as well, but not necessarily." He concludes that most American blacks, though racially mixed, are "physically distinguishable from whites, but they are also an ethnic group because of the distinctive culture they have developed within the general American framework." Such an inclusive definition suggests that the terms *black* and *mulatto* should be viewed as racial, cultural, and ethnic traits.

10. See United States Department of State, *Sixth Census* (Washington, D.C., 1841).

11. See Ira Berlin, "The Structure of the Free Negro Caste in the Antebellum United States," *Journal of Social History* 9 (Spring 1976): 305–311; Willard B. Gatewood, *Aristocrats of Color: The Black Elite, 1880–1920* (Bloomington: Indiana University Press, 1990), 7–29; and James Oliver Horton, *Free People of Color: Inside the African American Community* (Washington, D.C.: Smithsonian Institute, 1993), 122–144. It is also important to note that at least one historian refutes the theory that mulattos were considered superior to black slaves or that they

constituted a separate caste. See Eugene Genovese, *Roll Jordan, Roll: The World the Slaveholders Made* (New York: Pantheon, 1974).

12. John Hope Franklin, *From Slavery to Freedom: A History of Negro Americans*, 5th ed. (New York: Knopf, 1980), 148–149.

13. Larson, *Bound for the Promised Land*, 63.

14. Larson, *Bound for the Promised Land*, 327–328, n. 91.

15. Larson, *Bound for the Promised Land*, 64.

16. Catherine Clinton, *Harriet Tubman: The Road to Freedom* (New York: Little, Brown, 2004), 31.

17. Tubman, quoted in Sarah H. Bradford, *Scenes in the Life of Harriet Tubman* (Auburn, NY: W. J. Moses, 1869), 14–15.

18. Larson, *Bound for the Promised Land*, 73.

19. Tubman, quoted in Bradford, *Scenes in the Life*, 15.

20. Clinton, *Road to Freedom*, 31–32; and Larson, *Bound for the Promised Land*, 74–77.

21. Tubman, quoted in Sarah H. Bradford, *Harriet Tubman: The Moses of Her People* (1886; reprint, Secaucus, NJ: Citadel Press, 1961), 29.

22. Larson, *Bound for the Promised Land*, 78.

23. Notice of reward placed by Eliza Ann Brodess, *Cambridge Democrat* (Cambridge, Maryland): October 3, 1849.

24. Earl Conrad, *Harriet Tubman* (New York: Paul S. Eriksson, 1943), 30–33.

25. Stampp, *Peculiar Institution*, 110; Franklin, *From Slavery to Freedom*, 191; Genovese, *Roll Jordan, Roll*, 648; Franklin and Schweninger, *Runaway Slaves: Rebels on the Plantation*, 209–233; and James and Lois Horton, *Slavery and the Making of America*, 129

26. Bordewich, *Bound for Canaan*, 349.

27. Bradford, *Moses of Her People*, 27–28.

28. Bradford, *Scenes in the Life of Tubman*, 19.

29. Humez, *Harriet Tubman*, 16; and Bordewich, *Bound for Canaan*, 349.

30. Clinton, *Road to Freedom*, 38; Humez, *Harriet Tubman*, 18.

31. William C. Kashatus, *Just Over the Line: Chester County and the Underground Railroad* (University Park, PA: Penn State Press, 2002), 19–21.

32. Bradford, *Scenes in the Life of Tubman*, 20.

33. Bradford, *Scenes in the Life of Tubman*, 20.

34. James Oliver Horton and Lois E. Horton, *In Hope of Liberty: Culture, Community and Protest Among Northern Free Blacks, 1700–1860* (New York: Oxford University Press, 1997), 141; and Richard Allen, *The Life Experience and Gospel Labor of the Right Reverend Richard Allen* (1887; reprint, New York: Abingdon Press, 1960).

35. Humez, *Harriet Tubman*, 18; and Bordewich, *Bound for Canaan*, 350.

36. "Runaways," *Easton Star* (Easton, Maryland): August 14, 1849.

37. See David M. Potter, *The Impending Crisis, 1848–1861* (New York: Harper & Row, 1976), 26–42.

38. See Eric Foner, *Free Soil, Free Labor, Free Men: The Ideology of the Republican Party before the Civil War* (New York: Oxford University Press, 1970), 149–162.

39. See Bruce Levine, *Half Slave and Half Free: The Roots of the Civil War* (New York: Hill & Wang, 1992), 160–167.

40. See "The Fugitive Slave Bill of 1850," text quoted in William Still, *The Underground Railroad* (1871, reprinted by Johnson Publishing Company, Chicago, 1970), 355–360.

41. Horton, *Slavery and Making of America*, 148–149.

42. Larson, *Bound for the Promised Land*, 89–90; and Bordewich, *Bound for Canaan*, 344–346.

43. Larson, *Bound for the Promised Land*, 90.

Chapter 3

MOSES OF HER PEOPLE, 1851–1853

The Fugitive Slave Law emboldened Harriet Tubman to fight her own battle against the institution of slavery. What began as a personal desire for freedom quickly became a lifelong mission to free enslaved members of her family as well as other slaves who sought passage to the north. Historians speculate that the number of trips Tubman made to the South range between 10 and 19, and the number of runaway slaves she guided, between 70 and 300.[1] In addition, she is said to have commanded a reward estimated at between $12,000 and $40,000.[2] Regardless of the actual numbers, Tubman's place in American history as the predominant African American agent of the Underground Railroad was established by contemporaries who equated her with Moses, the Old Testament emancipator of the Hebrews.[3]

The Underground Railroad was the name used for the clandestine movement of African American slaves escaping out of the South with the assistance of a loosely organized network of abolitionists who aided them in their search for freedom in the North. While the enterprise began sometime after 1780 with the gradual abolition of slavery in Pennsylvania, the Underground Railroad was most active between 1835 and 1860. The abolitionists who operated the secret route adopted the vocabulary of the railroad to disguise its illegal activity. Accordingly, the term *underground* suggested invisibility, and *railroad*, a method of transportation. Those who opened their homes to runaways were referred to as *station masters*, and their homes were known as *stations*. Those who guided fugitives between stations were called *conductors*. Supporters called *stockholders* played a less dangerous—and less conspicuous—role, but one that was extremely important: they provided the finances needed for bribes, transportation, food, and clothing. *Agent* was a less specific term, referring to *anyone* who worked on the Underground Railroad.[4]

Agents formed *vigilance committees* that would gather intelligence on the movement of owners and slave catchers who were tracking fugitives as well as to give succor to runaways. Some even snatched captured fugitives directly from the arms of federal marshals, rushed them to places of hiding, and then ultimately to safety and freedom. Whether station masters, conductors, or stockholders, participants on the Underground Railroad were black and white, male and female, free and slave. They also came from a range of economic backgrounds, political persuasions, and religious faiths, reflecting the fact that the movement was based, more than anything else, on individual conscience.[5]

Most often, runaways escaped to the North using a loose network of routes through the border states. Two of the most heavily traveled routes were the Eastern and Mid-Western Lines. The Mid-Western Line originated in southwestern Ohio, attracting slaves from the Deep South as well as the Upper South states of Kentucky and Tennessee. This route took fugitives across the Ohio River to a number of routes through Ohio, Indiana, and Illinois into Canada. The Eastern Line, on the other hand, originated in Maryland and extended through Pennsylvania into New York, New England, and on into Canada. Runaways using the Eastern Line often headed into such cities as Philadelphia, New York, and Boston with the hope of assimilating into the free black community. Some fugitives stowed away on ships and escaped up the coast with the hope of arriving in either Massachusetts or Maine, which were free states. Others continued on to Canada, which routinely refused U.S. requests for the slaves' return.[6]

Tubman's involvement came on the Underground Railroad's Eastern Line, especially with the network of abolitionists who comprised the Chesapeake Route, which originated on the Delaware-Maryland-

Virginia—or Delmarva—Peninsula. Black oyster men, shipyard and dock workers, and wagon drivers among others provided Tubman and the fugitives she guided with intelligence, safe houses, and escape routes into Delaware and eventually to the free state of Pennsylvania.[7] This was the route Harriet used in the autumn of 1851 when she returned to the Eastern Shore to rescue her husband, John. She had planned the journey for months in advance, sending word to him that she wanted him to join her in Philadelphia. She had saved money from various jobs and even purchased a new suit of clothes for him. When she arrived in Dorchester County, however, she discovered that John had taken another wife, a free woman by the name of Caroline. Harriet did not dare venture into Caroline's presence. Instead she sent word to her husband where she was, but he refused to join her. Devastated by the rejection, Harriet was determined to "go right in and make all the trouble she could," regardless of the consequences. But after reconsidering, she decided she could "do without him" and "dropped [him] out of her heart."[8] Instead, she found a group of 11 slaves who wanted to escape.

Few details about this escape are known. Questions remain about whether these were the same fugitives Harriet rescued in the autumn of 1851, or another group she rescued from the Eastern Shore in December 1851. Frederick Douglass, one of the most respected antislavery journalists, suggested that Tubman en route from New York City to Canada sought shelter for the group with him at Rochester, New York. Douglass, who escaped slavery in 1838, had relocated at Rochester in 1847, where he founded *The North Star*, an antislavery newspaper. He also opened his home as a station along the same Underground Railroad route Tubman traveled between Philadelphia and Canada. In his autobiography, *Life and Times of Frederick Douglass*, the African American agent describes what may have been Harriet's visit in December 1851:

On one occasion I had eleven fugitives at the same time under my roof, and it was necessary for them to remain with me until I could collect sufficient money to get them to Canada. It was the largest number I ever had at any one time, and I had some difficulty in providing so many with food and shelter, but, as may well be imagined, they were not very fastidious in either direction, and were well content with very plain food, and a strip of carpet on the floor for a bed, or a place on the straw in the barnloft.[9]

It is important to note that Douglass could not reveal the names of the fugitives or the other agents on the Underground Railroad. To do so would place them in severe danger with the civil authorities. But there is no doubt that Tubman knew and relied on Douglass's assistance whenever she was conducting a group of fugitives through upstate New York. Harriet stated that fact herself, admitting that whenever she traveled from New York City to Canada, she passed through Rochester "where the fugitive slave Frederick Douglass would see that she got on the train for the Suspension Bridge and St. Catharines in Canada."[10] Douglass was a great admirer of Tubman's. In a letter to Harriet, written at the request of Sarah Bradford for her first biography Tubman in 1868, Douglass praised Tubman's selflessness and courage on behalf of the many slaves she guided to freedom:

You ask for what you do not need when you call upon me for a word of commendation. I need such words from you far more than you can need them from me, especially where your superior labors and devotion to the cause of the lately enslaved of our land are known as I know them. The difference between us is very marked. Most that I have done and suffered in the service of our cause has been public, and I have received much encouragement at every step of the way. You, on the other hand, have labored in a private way. I have wrought in the day—you in the night. . . . The midnight sky and the silent stars have been the witnesses of your heroism. . . . I know of no one who has willingly encountered more perils and hardships to serve our enslaved people than you have.[11]

After being rebuffed by her husband, Harriet vowed "to give her life to brave deeds."[12] Perhaps her separation from John Tubman reinforced her decision to dedicate her life to helping others in bondage. Motherhood was not a possibility now, if it ever was. If Harriet had doubts about her life's journey, she would resolve them with God's help. "Long ago when the Lord told me to go free my people I said, 'No, Lord! I can't go. Don't ask me,'" she explained years later. "But He came another time, and I said again, 'Lord, go away. Get some better-educated person. Get a person with more culture than I have.' But He came back a third time, and spoke to me just as he did to Moses. He said, 'Harriet, I want you.' And I knew then I must do what He bid me to do."[13] Still, she was embarking on an extremely dangerous career.

African Americans, both free and slave, responded to the Fugitive Slave Act with increasing violence. On February 15, 1851, a runaway known as Shadrach was arrested in Boston and taken to the courthouse. Some 50 Negroes rushed into the hearing and fought off federal marshals in order to free the fugitive, who was rushed off to Canada. Two months later, Boston's municipal government had to turn out 300 soldiers to guard another runaway slave, Thomas Sims, from being rescued by abolitionists.[14] A more horrific event unfolded on the farmlands of Lancaster County, Pennsylvania.

On September 11, 1851, William Parker, a resident of Christiana, Pennsylvania, and a free black station master, was confronted by Edward Gorsuch, a Baltimore slaveholder and a small party that included his son and a deputy U.S. marshal. Gorsuch believed that Parker was harboring three of his slaves who had recently escaped. When the belligerent slaveholder tried to gain entry into the house, Parker's wife sounded a horn to summon help. A band of local free blacks responded to the call. Threats were exchanged. When it was clear that the blacks would not yield to their demands, the slave catchers began to attack the house. The blacks stood their ground, defending themselves with whatever weapons they could muster. When the smoke cleared, the fugitives had escaped, Gorsuch was dead, his son was gravely injured, and the others had run off in fear. Parker escaped to Canada on the Underground Railroad, insisting that Africans in the United States had "no country" because they had no protection under the law. Thirty other free blacks who participated in the Christiana Riot were tried for treason, but Pennsylvania Congressman Thaddeus Stevens so ably defended them that the jury returned a "not guilty" verdict in 15 minutes.[15] Such violent incidents registered the need for better organization among black and white Underground Railroad agents.

On December 2, 1852, the Pennsylvania Antislavery Society, located in Philadelphia, responded to the need by creating a General Vigilance Committee of 19 persons. Four members of the group formed an acting committee headed by William Still, the self-educated son of former slaves.[16] Still raised funds, corresponded with station masters and conductors, and coordinated the movements along the Eastern Line of the Underground Railroad. He stocked a veritable storehouse of food and clothing for runaways at his office at 31 North Fifth Street, and, with the help of the vigilance committee, aided in many daring escapes.[17] After the passage of the Fugitive Slave Law, vigilance committees began to emerge in many Northern cities. The committees were the most structured vehicles of the Underground Railroad. In Philadelphia, working–class blacks served as the backbone of the vigilance committee. Free blacks sheltered and transported fugitives as well as gathered and relayed crucial information to Still. Others kept watch for suspicious whites they observed in the hotels or boardinghouses, or on the streets of the city. Many of the vigilance committee members belonged to Mother Bethel, the city's oldest and largest African Methodist Episcopal church, organized in 1794 by the Reverend Richard Allen, a former Delaware slave.[18] Acting from a sense of personal obligation to their enslaved brethren, Philadelphia's free black community raised the bulk of the vigilance committee's operating funds from African American benevolent societies and A.M.E. church-affiliated auxiliaries.[19] Their success is reflected in the hundreds of runaways they assisted, which has been estimated at 495 between December 1852 and February 1857.[20]

As director of Philadelphia's General Vigilance Committee, William Still not only coordinated the Eastern Line of the Underground Railroad by finding shelter and escape routes to the North for fugitive slaves, but he also recorded their heart-wrenching stories of inhumane treatment and brutality by callous owners, painful family separations, and their passionate desire for freedom.[21] Still played an instrumental role in Tubman's success as a conductor and described, at length, her method of operation in his seminal book, *The Underground Railroad*, published in 1872:

Harriet Tubman had been the [slaves'] "Moses." She had faithfully gone down into Egypt, and had delivered bondmen by her own heroism. Harriet was a woman of no pretensions, indeed, a more ordinary specimen of humanity could hardly be found among the most unfortunate-looking farm hands of the South. Yet, in point of

William Still (1819 or 1821–1902), secretary of the Vigilance Committee of Philadelphia, who coordinated the Eastern Line of the Underground Railroad. From the frontispiece to Still's The Underground Railroad *(Philadelphia: Porter and Coates, 1872). (Courtesy of the Chester County Historical Society, West Chester, PA)*

courage, shrewdness and disinterested exertions to rescue her fellow-men, by making personal visits to Maryland among the slaves, she was without her equal. Her success was wonderful.

Time and again she made successful visits to Maryland on the Underground Rail Road, and would be absent for weeks at a time, running daily risks while making preparations for herself and passengers. Great fears were entertained for her safety, but she seemed wholly devoid of personal fear. The idea of being captured by slave-hunters or slave-holders, seemed never to enter her mind. She was apparently proof against all adversaries. While she thus manifested such utter personal indifference, she was much more watchful with regard to those she was piloting.

Half of her time, she had the appearance of one asleep, and would actually sit down by the road-side and go fast asleep when on her errands of mercy through the South, yet, she would not suffer one of her party to whimper once, about "giving out and going back," however wearied they might be from hard travel day and night. She had a very short and pointed rule or law of her own, which implied death to any who talked of giving out and going back. Thus, in an emergency she would give all to understand that "times were very critical and therefore no foolishness would be indulged in on the road." That several who were rather weak-kneed and faint-hearted were greatly invigorated by Harriet's blunt and positive manner and threat of extreme measures, there could be no doubt. After having once enlisted, "they had to go through or die . . ."

Of course Harriet was supreme, and her followers generally had full faith in her, and would back up any word she might utter. So when she said to them that "a live runaway could do great harm by going back, but that a dead one could tell no secrets," she was sure to have obedience. Therefore, none had to die as traitors on the "middle passage." It is obvious enough, however, that her success in going into Maryland as she did, was attributable to her adventurous spirit and utter disregard of consequences. Her like it is probable was never known before or since.[22]

Since the Underground Railroad operated in secrecy, many basic facts about its operation are either unknown or shrouded in a mix of historical fact and legend, embellished by more than 150 years of folklore. But some of the existing documentary evidence has allowed historians to determine the routes used by Tubman in guiding fugitive slaves to the north.[23]

Tubman acted exclusively on the upper part of the Underground Railroad's Eastern Line, specifically between northern Virginia and Canada. Her rescue missions took place along two major routes: the Chesapeake Route and the Overland Route. Each route contained various secondary routes that enabled her to change course because of the ever-present dangers involved in conducting slaves, including the close proximity of slave catchers, information of impending dangers supplied by friends, or instructions she received from the spiritual world while in trance.

THE CHESAPEAKE ROUTE

The Chesapeake Route began in Tubman's native city of Cambridge in Dorchester County, Maryland. From here, Harriet traveled by boat on the Chesapeake Bay to Baltimore. After her arrival in the city, she could find refuge with Tom Tubman, her brother-in-law, and with friends of his family. Other sanctuaries she used included the Orchard Street African Methodist Episcopal (A.M.E.) Church, which served as both a place of worship as well as a refuge for runaways.[24] From Baltimore, Harriet could continue north on the Chesapeake, secreted on a steamship by African American stewards, until she reached the Chesapeake & Delaware Canal. She would then sail east on the canal to its terminus at Delaware City. If she was able to disembark there undetected, she could travel north, on foot, 20 miles to Wilmington, Delaware, to the home of Quaker station master Thomas Garrett. Alternatively, Harriet could remain on board the ship, bypass Garrett's station, and continue north on the Delaware River until she reached Philadelphia.[25]

Another option Harriet could exercise after reaching Baltimore was to avoid the C & D Canal altogether and sail due north to Havre de Grace, the city where the Susquehanna River empties into Chesapeake Bay. Once at Havre de Grace, she could cross northeast Maryland and travel on foot into southern Lancaster County, Pennsylvania. If slave catchers were on her trail once she crossed into the Keystone State, Harriet could continue north on the Susquehanna River until she reached a point parallel to the town of Peach Bottom and proceed eastward into Chester County. Alternatively, she could continue north, on the Susquehanna or by foot, until she reached the city of Columbia, Lancaster County. There she could avoid detection by seeking sanctuary with Quaker stationmaster Daniel Gibbons, or free black agents William Whipper, Stephen Smith, Elweed Brown, Henry Bushong, and Robert Loney.[26]

From Lancaster County, Harriet proceeded northeast toward Philadelphia. Once she arrived in the City of Brotherly Love, Harriet's first stop would be the home of William Still, the coordinator of the Eastern Line. Philadelphia was the destination of choice for many fugitives, who began their life in freedom by assimilating into the city's considerable free black population. If they decided to continue northward, fugitives received assistance from many Quaker agents who lived in the city, including Lucretia Mott, founder of the Female Anti-slavery Society and a close friend of Tubman's.[27]

Once she left Philadelphia, Harriet had to make a decision whether to travel northeast across New Jersey to New York City, or west to Reading, Pennsylvania. Her decision was determined, as always, by the pursuit of slave catchers, and the need for shelter, food, shoes, and general assistance. If she decided to travel west toward central Pennsylvania, Harriet and her passengers could find refuge at Reading's Bethel A.M.E. Church. Reading was also a major rail center and many fugitives were hidden on freight and baggage cars and forwarded to Elmira, New York, where John W. Jones, a former slave, would receive them.[28] Jones guided them to the station of Reverend Samuel Perry, pastor of the African American Episcopal Zion Church at Ithaca.[29]

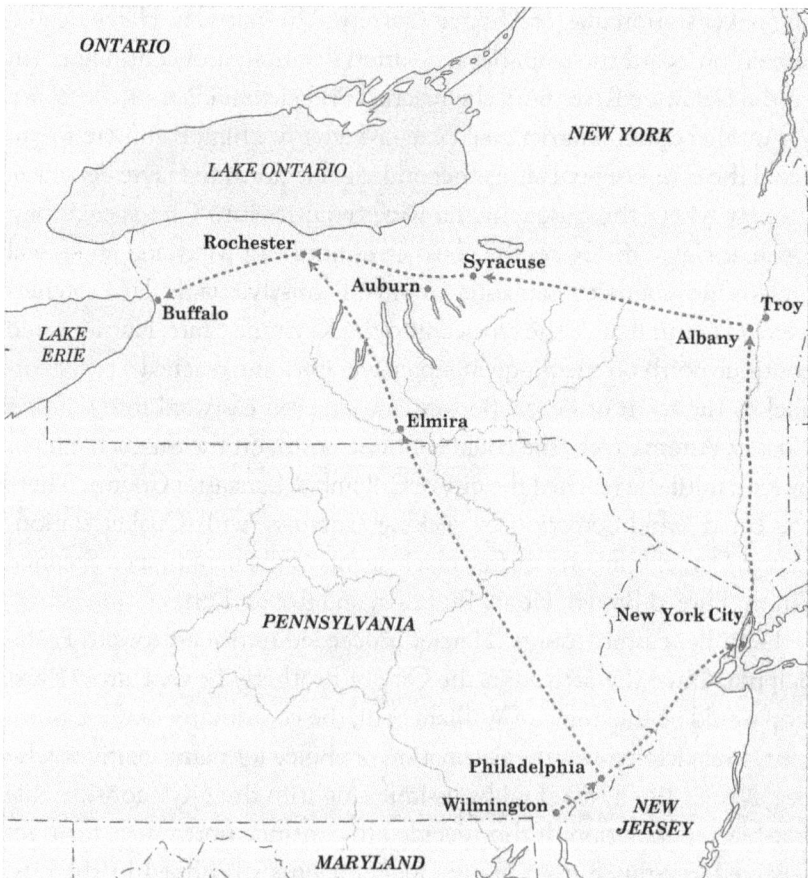

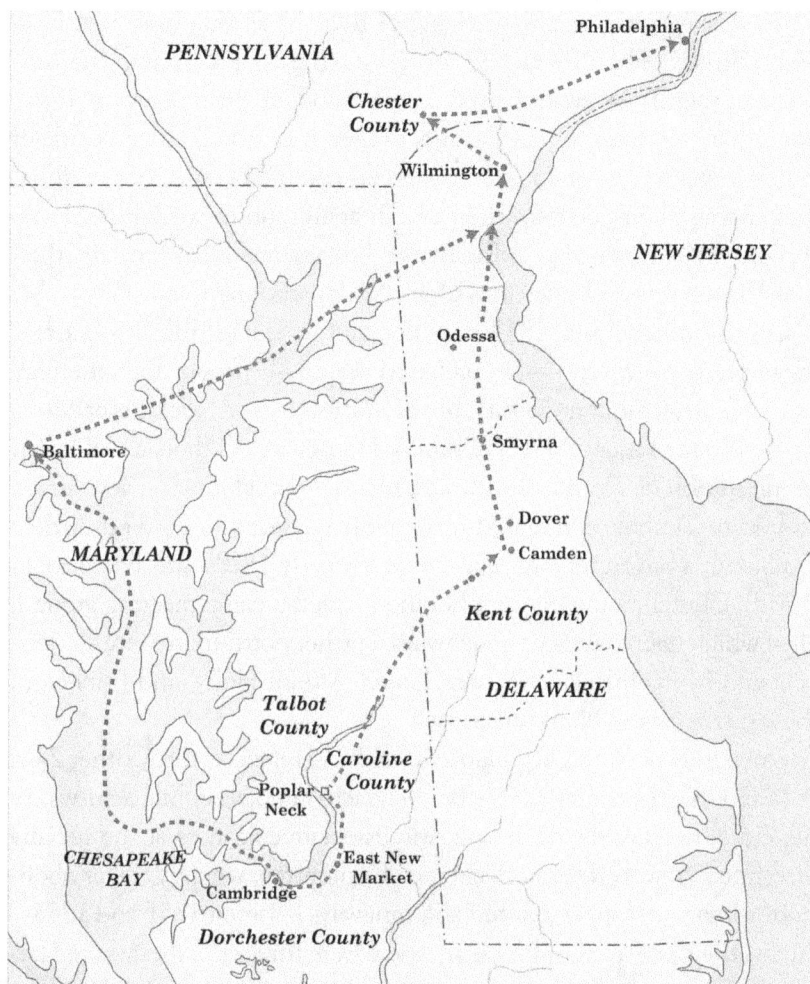

Maps of Harriet Tubman's Underground Railroad routes. She was active on the northern portion of the Eastern Line and varied her primary and secondary routes according to circumstances and reports she received about the activities of slave catchers and other dangers. (Courtesy of Michael Dolan)

From Ithaca, Harriet traveled north to the city of Auburn, just above the five Finger Lakes in northern New York State. Auburn was the home of William H. Seward, an influential United States Senator and a radical opponent of slavery who would later become President Abraham Lincoln's Secretary of State. Seward and his wife, Frances Adeline, hid runaway slaves in the upstairs wing of their large, two-story house on South Street. When there were no guests, the couple invited the runaways to spend time with them downstairs and all dined together. There was also a Negro settlement known as New Guinea on the east side of Auburn where Harriet and her passengers could be assured of rest, food, shelter, and other needs for their still difficult journey to Canada. From Auburn, Harriet traveled to Rochester, Buffalo, and Lewiston. She then took the suspension bridge into Ontario, Canada, and freedom.[30]

On the other hand, if Harriet decided to leave Philadelphia and travel across New Jersey—her preferred route—she would find sanctuary at Lawnside, Camden County, at the station of free black Peter Mott, or the Mount Pisgah A.M.E. Church. Harriet would then travel north to the station of Thomas and Josiah Evans at Haddonfield, New Jersey, and on to Timbuktu, named for the fabled desert city in West Africa. Timbuktu, a haven for runaways since the early 1820s, was home to an A.M.E. Church, a free black schoolhouse, and a camp meeting ground, all of which offered refuge to runaways. Further north there were stations operated by free blacks at Mount Laurel, Mount Holly, and Princeton, the last stop before New York City.[31]

Once in New York City, Harriet could find refuge at the Mother Zion A.M.E. Church; the office of the *National Anti-Slavery Standard* where her close friend, Oliver Johnson, was associate editor; or at the racially integrated New York State Vigilance Committee, where Quaker abolitionist Isaac T. Hopper assisted 686 runaways between 1851 and 1853.[32] Across the East River, in Brooklyn, there were three churches where Harriet could stop: the Bridge Street African Methodist Episcopal Wesleyan Church, the Siloam Presbyterian Church, and the Plymouth Church of the Pilgrims.[33]

Tubman traveled from New York City up the Hudson River to the state capitol at Albany. At various times, she chose to travel by foot, stagecoach, railroad, and boat. It was the least dangerous passageway of the entire Underground Railroad because of the Hudson's sparsely settled banks and the scarcity of slave hunters. From Albany, Harriet journeyed to Troy, New York, relying on the black minister Henry Highland Garnet for assistance. Continuing west, Harriet stopped at Peterboro, New York, where she stayed with Gerrit Smith, a leading social reformer and one of Tubman's most important benefactors. From Smith's station, Harriet traveled northwest to Syracuse, New York, where she was welcomed by either the free black agent Jermain Wesley Loguen or Samuel J. May, a Unitarian clergyman.[34]

Continuing west toward Canada, Harriet's next stop was Auburn, where she stayed with William Seward, or with free black agents who settled the New Guinea community. From Auburn, Harriet traveled to Rochester, home to the great black orator Frederick Douglass. Douglass, who also escaped bondage on Maryland's Eastern Shore, operated a popular station for runaways on Alexander Street in Rochester.[35] On one occasion, Tubman brought 11 fugitives to him and Douglass admitted they were "the largest number [he] ever had at any one time" and that he "had some difficulty in providing so many with food and shelter."[36] When Harriet was not staying with Douglass she could finder shelter with the family of women's suffragist Susan B. Anthony, or Isaac and Amy Post, a white Quaker couple.[37]

From Rochester, Harriet traveled to Buffalo, located at the confluence of Lake Erie, and the Niagara and Buffalo rivers. There she met with William Wells Brown, a runaway slave from Lexington, Kentucky, who smuggled runaways aboard steamships bound for Canada.[38] Alternatively, Tubman could elect to stop at Lewistown, which was on the United States side of the Niagara River from Canada and the last stop before freedom. She would then cross over the famous suspension bridge, built in 1848 to connect Niagara Falls, New York, with Niagara Falls, Canada. Several stations were located there, including the home of Reverend Amos Tyron, the Riverside Inn on Water Street, and the Niagara Frontier Bible Church on Mohawk and River Roads. Fugitives found sanctuary at these places until boat transportation could be arranged for them to cross the Niagara River.[39]

For many fugitives, Ontario, Canada, was the ultimate destination because it had abolished slavery in 1833. Tubman's route took her across the Suspension Bridge into the town of St. Catharines, Ontario. Once she arrived in the Canadian town, she headed directly for the British Methodist Episcopal Church and Salem Chapel at the corner of Geneva and North streets, the final terminus on the Underground Railroad. Harriet was a member of this church, and used it as a sanctuary for the slaves she rescued. From here, fugitives adjusted to their new lives in freedom in one of Ontario's many communities of former slaves.[40]

THE OVER LAND ROUTE

Harriet's second major route was over land, which also began on Maryland's Eastern Shore, specifically in Dorchester, Talbot, and Caroline counties.[41] From here, Harriet guided runaways to the northeast along the Choptank River into Delaware. On this route she relied heavily on Samuel Green, a free black minister who lived on East New Market, Maryland; Francis S. Corkran, a white Quaker agent living in Cambridge; and her parents, who lived at Poplar Neck in Caroline County.

Once she reached Kent County, Delaware, Tubman enjoyed several options. She could stay at one of many stations operated by free blacks, who included Samuel D. Burris, William Brinkly, Nat Brinkly, Joe Finney, and Abraham Gibbs near Camden, Delaware. Alternatively, Harriet could find refuge with Quaker stationmasters Ezekial Jenkins and John Hunn.[42] Continuing north, she might stop at the Dover station of Henry Cowgill, a Quaker agent, or Smyrna where Daniel Corbet would offer her refuge, or further north at Odessa, where the Appoquinimink Friend's Meeting House was located.[43] From there, she was able to cross the Chesapeake and Delaware Canal to Wilmington, which afforded a relatively safe environment.

Wilmington was located a short distance from the Pennsylvania boundary and freedom. It was also home to one of the most fearless Underground Railroad agents, Thomas Garrett, and several free black conductors, including Severn Johnson, Harry Craig, Comegys Munson, Joseph Hamilton, and Joseph G. Walker.[44] Their objective was to transport fugitives into Chester County, Pennsylvania, a hotbed of Underground Railroad activity located just over the Mason-Dixon Line dividing the free and slave states. Once she reached Chester County, Harriet had two options. She could send runaways due north to William Still in Philadelphia, or west to the home of Elijah Pennypacker in Phoenixville. Pennypacker would then forward the fugitives to Allen and Maria Agnew in Norristown, who in turn would send them on to the City of Brotherly Love.[45] At Philadelphia, William Still, the coordinator of the Eastern Line, would help Tubman channel the fugitives northward to safer locations using the same routes through New Jersey and New York as described above.

UNDERGROUND RAILROAD FOLKLORE

While the routes Harriet Tubman used to guide runaways northward to freedom can be documented, some of her other methods of escape are rooted in folklore. The folklore of the Underground Railroad is based on the oral culture and traditions of the African American people and consists of customs, songs, stories, and tangible objects like quilts.[46] Some of the folklore is embellished, being spun from popular anecdotes designed to boost the pride of a small town or community. But since most slaves could not read or write, they were dependent on oral tradition to tell their stories as a means of passing their history on to the next generation. Thus, while the folklore of the Underground Railroad is sometimes controversial because it lacks written documentation, oral tradition suggests that Harriet Tubman relied on such folklore in conducting fugitives to the north.[47]

Spirituals and popular slave songs, for example, were believed to be used by black conductors and slaves as a covert method of communication to plan escapes.[48] Accordingly, field slaves sang the spiritual "Go Down Moses" to announce Harriet's arrival on Maryland's Eastern Shore for those who planned to escape:

When Israel was in Egypt's land,
Let my people go.
Oppressed so hard they could not stand,
Let my people go.
Go down Moses, way down in Egypt's land.
Tell ole pharaoh,
Let my people go.

Although the spiritual sounds like the innocent recounting of a popular biblical story, "Go Down Moses," when sung by slaves, contained a secret code. The name Moses not only referred to the Old Testament leader who led the Israelites out of bondage in Egypt, but also to Harriet Tubman, the so-called Moses of her people, or black slaves. Pharaoh was the slaveholder. Egypt was the South, where Tubman would travel to guide her people out of bondage and to freedom in the Promised Land of the North.[49] In addition to the code words, the verse had a special message. If slave catchers were nearby and it was too dangerous for Harriet to attempt the escape, she would sing the rather ominous verse twice:

> Moses go down in Egypt,
> Tell ole pharaoh let me go;
> Hadn't been for Adam's fall,
> Shouldn't had to die at all.

Once the danger had passed, Harriet sang the more joyous refrain:

> Oh go down, Moses,
> Way down into Egypt's land,
> Tell old Pharaoh,
> Let my people go.
> Oh Pharaoh said he would go cross
> Let my people go,
> And don't get lost in the wilderness,
> Let my people go.
> Oh go down, Moses,
> Way down into Egypt's land,
> Tell old Pharaoh,
> Let my people go.
> You may hinder me here, but you can't up there,
> Let my people go.
> He sits in Heaven and answers prayers,
> Let my people go!

> Oh go down, Moses,
> Way down into Egypt's land,
> Tell old Pharaoh
> Let my people go.[50]

"I'm Bound for the Promised Land" was one of Harriet's favorite hymns and one also used to signal slaves that she was in the area on another rescue mission:

When that old Chariot comes
I'm going to leave you
I'm bound for the Promised Land
I'm going to leave you.
I'm sorry, I'm going to leave you
Farewell, Oh farewell
But I'll meet you in the morning
Farewell, Oh farewell.
I'll meet you in the morning.

I'm bound for the Promised Land
On the other side of Jordan
I'm bound for the Promised Land
I'll meet you in the morning.
Safe in the Promised Land
On the other side of Jordan
Bound for the Promise Land.

The bittersweet hymn, with its alternating references to the sadness of departure and the joy of traveling to freedom in the North, acknowledged the mixed emotions of leaving family and friends for a better life "on the other side of Jordan." The hymn also offered practical advice. It signaled the departure time as "morning," which meant in the darkness of the early morning—not daybreak. The cover of darkness would not only conceal the escape but also offer a head start before the master learned of it.[51]

"Follow the Drinking Gourd" was another popular song that gave practical advice for finding the way to freedom and one that was supposedly used by Tubman.

Follow the drinking gourd,
follow the drinking gourd
For the old man is a-waiting to carry
us to freedom
Follow the drinking gourd.
When the sun goes down and the
first quail calls
Follow the drinking gourd

"Follow the Drinking Gourd" was a secret metaphor for the Big Dipper, a constellation of stars that resembles a gourd used to dip water from a bucket. The two stars on the outer side of the bowl point to the North Star, the only star whose position in the sky is fixed. By waiting until "the sun goes down" and going in the direction of the North Star, runaways headed north toward freedom. When she first escaped from slavery in 1849, Harriet, like many fugitives, did not know whom to trust as she traveled across unfamiliar terrain. But by following the North Star she knew she would eventually reach free territory. The song served as a reminder for her passengers that, if separated from her, they should rely on the North Star to guide them to freedom.[52]

By 1853, Harriet Tubman had established a residence in Philadelphia where she supported herself as a hotel cook and laundress. In the summer months, Harriet worked as a cook and maid at the oceanfront hotels in Cape May, New Jersey. Most of the income she earned was saved for her journeys back to the Eastern Shore to liberate family members.[53] Harriet usually conducted her rescue missions during the winter months when the nights were long and station masters would be at home waiting for her arrival. Once she made contact with slaves who wanted to escape, she would leave on a Saturday evening since the newspapers would not print runaway notices until Monday morning.[54] Harriet also maintained a strong network of abolitionist friends. In addition to William Still and the free black members of the city's General Vigilance Committee, she was associated with James and Lucretia Mott, white Quaker antislavery and women's rights activists whom she described as people who "stood behind [fugitive slaves] when there was no one else."[55] The Motts, who later relocated to a farmhouse north of the city, were also active on the Underground Railroad and frequently gave sanctuary to Harriet during her rescue missions.[56]

Tubman's appreciation for the efforts of northern white abolitionists had its limits, though. She expressed no desire, for example, to learn more about Harriet Beecher Stowe's novel, Uncle Tom's Cabin, which was based on actual slave experiences and brought the horrors of slavery to life for white readers. Stowe's work was initially published in serial form in an abolitionist newspaper. Then, in March 1852, it was published as a book and proved to be the most powerful of all abolitionist propaganda, selling more than 300,000 copies within a year of publication. Thousands of white northerners who were previously indifferent to slavery began to condemn it. This enormous new audience consisted not only of those who could read the book, but also those who watched countless theater companies reenact the story on stages across the nation.[57] When the play appeared in Philadelphia, Harriet, who was working at one of the city's large hotels, was asked by coworkers to go with them to see it. "No," said Harriet. "I haven't got no heart to go and see the suffering of my people played on the stage. I've heard some of 'Uncle Tom's Cabin' read, and I tell you Mrs. Stowe's pen hasn't begun to paint what slavery is as I have seen it at the far South. I've seen the real thing, and I don't want to see it on no stage or in no theater."[58]

Tubman's difficulty with Stowe's novel may have been due, in part, to her own self-righteousness. Having suffered the brutal experience of slavery herself, she took exception to a Northern white female's second-hand interpretation of it. Perhaps she mistook Stowe's sympathy for a white person's pretentiousness in believing that any white could actually empathize with the plight of a slave without having experienced the lash of the slave master. Despite her personal difficulty with Stowe and her novel, Harriet Tubman would be hard pressed to deny that her own success as a conductor was based, in part, on the assistance she received from white Northerners. Without them, she may not have become the "Moses of her people."

NOTES

1. Milton C. Sernett, *Harriet Tubman: Myth, Memory, and History* (Durham, NC: Duke University Press, 2007), 62–66.

2. Sernett, *Myth, Memory and History*, 66–67.

3. See Franklin B. Sanborn, "Harriet Tubman," *Commonwealth*: July 17, 1863; Rosa Belle Holt, "A Heroine in Ebony," *Chautauquan* 23 (July 1896): 461; and William Still, *Underground Railroad* (1872; reprinted, Chicago: Johnson, 1970), 305–306. It's not known when Harriet Tubman was first referred to as "Moses," but the appellation was an affectionate reference given to her by the slaves. She was also called "the Moses of her People" by abolitionist friends who knew of her promise to God to serve His oppressed creatures and had heard the stories she told them of her journeys into the South to rescue slaves.

4. John Hope Franklin, *From Slavery to Freedom: A History of Negro Americans*, 5th ed. (New York: Knopf, 1980), 189–194; and C. Peter Ripley, *Underground Railroad* (Washington, D.C.: United States Department of the Interior, 1998), 45–46. According to Larry Gara, "at least four writers have forwarded different versions of the term 'Underground Railroad.'" The most common story traces the term to the escape of a Kentucky slave named Tice David in 1831. When David reached the Ohio River and saw that his owner was in close pursuit, he jumped in the river and swam across. The owner pursued him in a boat but once he reached the shore the slave could not be found. Later, when asked what had become of his slave, the owner allegedly replied that "he must have gone off on an underground railroad." The first modern analysis of the Underground Railroad is Larry Gara, *The Liberty Line: The Legend of the Underground Railroad* (Lexington: University of Kentucky, 1961), 173–174.

5. Ripley, *Underground Railroad*, 45–46.

6. Ripley, *Underground Railroad*, 48, 54.

7. Still, *Underground Railroad*, 74, 297, 530–531; Wilbur H. Siebert, *The Underground Railroad: From Slavery to Freedom* (New York: Macmillan, 1898. Reprint, New York: Russell & Russell, 1967), 410–411; and William J. Switala, *Underground Railroad in Delaware, Maryland, and West Virginia* (Mechanicsburg, PA: Stackpole Books, 2004), 76–79.

8. Ednah D. Cheney, "Moses," *Freedmen's Record* (March 1865): 35. Although she would not remarry until after John's death some 16 years later, Harriet would retain the surname Tubman for the rest of her life.

9. Frederick Douglass, *The Life and Times of Frederick Douglass* (1881; reprint, London: Collier-Macmillan, 1969), 266.

10. Harriet Tubman, quoted by Siebert, *The Underground Railroad: From Slavery to Freedom*, 186–187.

11. Frederick Douglass, quoted by Sarah H. Bradford, *Scenes in the Life of Harriet Tubman* (Auburn, NY: W. J. Moses, 1869), 7.

12. Tubman, quoted in Jean Humez, *Harriet Tubman: The Life and the Life Stories* (Madison: University of Wisconsin, 2003), 538.

13. Tubman, quoted in Holt, "A Heroine in Ebony," 462.

14. Franklin B. Sanborn, "Harriet Tubman," *Boston Commonwealth*: July 17, 1863.

15. Thomas Slaughter, *Bloody Dawn: The Christiana Riot and Racial Violence in the Antebellum North* (New York: Oxford University Press, 1991). For a more Afrocentric treatment, see Ella Forbes, *But We Have No Country: The 1851 Christiana Resistance* (Cherry Hill, NJ: Africana Homestead Legacy Publishers, 1998).

16. Still, *Underground Railroad*, 365. William Still was the youngest of 18 children of a slave family. His father, after purchasing his own freedom, resettled in New Jersey and became a father. William's mother eventually rejoined her husband after a successful escape. In 1844, at the age of 22, William left his family and moved to Philadelphia. With only five dollars to his name and no friends, he met J. Miller McKim, editor of *The Pennsylvania Freeman*, an abolitionist newspaper. With McKim's assistance, Still learned how to read and write. Three years later, he took a job with the Pennsylvania Anti-Slavery Society.

17. Benjamin Quarles, Preface to Still, *Underground Railroad*, vi–vii.

18. Benjamin Quarles, *Black Abolitionists* (New York: Oxford University Press, 1969; Da Capo paperback edition, 1991), 154–155; and Gary B. Nash, *Forging Freedom: The Formation of Philadelphia's Black Community, 1720–1840* (Cambridge, MA: Harvard University, 1988), 265–267. The predecessor of the Pennsylvania Anti-Slavery Society's General Vigilance Committee was the Philadelphia Vigilance Committee, founded in 1838. Though interracial in membership, only 2 of the 13 members of the standing committee were African American: Robert Purvis, the president; and Jacob C. White. After 1839, the white members stopped attending the monthly meetings of the committee and it became an exclusively black operation. Between 1839 and 1844, when the organization disbanded, the Philadelphia Vigilance Committee assisted some 300 fugitives each year. See Joseph A. Borome, "The Vigilant Committee of Philadelphia," *Pennsylvania Magazine of History and Biography*, 92 (July 1968): 320–351.

19. James O. Horton and Lois E. Horton, *In Hope of Liberty: Culture, Community and Protest among Northern Free Blacks, 1700–1860.* (New York: Oxford University, 1997), 230.

20. Quarles, *Black Abolitionists*, 156.

21. See Still, *Underground Railroad*. Between 1853 and 1860, Still recorded the personal histories of nearly 1,000 runaways. Fearing that the

records might be "captured by a pro-slavery mob," he hid them in a Philadelphia cemetery and kept subsequent notes of his interviews "on loose slips of paper." In 1872, Still published the records of 847 runaways in a 780-page book titled, *The Underground Railroad*. Another 149 cases are contained in a separate "Journal C" which was never published but can be found in manuscript form at the Historical Society of Pennsylvania in Philadelphia. A statistical analysis of the 996 runaway slaves assisted by Still was completed by James A. McGowan and William C. Kashatus, *Angel at Philadelphia: A Study of William Still's Underground Railroad* (unpublished manuscript).

22. Still, *Underground Railroad*, 305–306.

23. Most of what we know about the various routes of the Underground Railroad come from the following sources: Robert C. Smedley, M.D., *History of the Underground Railroad in Chester and the Neighboring Counties of Pennsylvania* (Lancaster, PA: Office of *The Journal*, 1883; reprint, Arno Press and *The New York Times*, 1969); Wilbur Siebert, *The Underground Railroad: From Slavery to Freedom*; Charles L. Blockson, *Hippocrene Guide to the Underground Railroad* (New York: Hippocrene Books, 1994); Bruce Chadwick, *Traveling the Underground Railroad* (Secaucus, NJ: Citadel Press, 1999); William J. Switala, *Underground Railroad in Pennsylvania* (Mechanicsburg, PA: Stackpole Books, 2001); and Switala, *Underground Railroad in Delaware, Maryland and West Virginia* (Mechanicsburg, PA: Stackpole Books, 2004).

24. Blockson, *Hippocrene Guide*, 42.

25. Switala, *Underground Railroad in Delaware, Maryland*, 81–85.

26. Smedley, *Chester County Underground Railroad*, 29, 77–78; and Switala, *Underground Railroad in Pennsylvania*, 123–127.

27. Benjamin Quarles, *Black Abolitionists* (New York: Da Capo, 1969), 26; and Switala, *Underground Railroad in Pennsylvania*, 141–151.

28. Chadwick, *Traveling the Underground Railroad*, 160.

29. Blockson, *Hippocrene Guide*, 73.

30. Chadwick, *Traveling the Underground Railroad*, 177–183.

31. Blockson, *Hippocrene Guide*, 50–54.

32. Blockson, *Hippocrene Guide*, 154.

33. Blockson, *Hippocrene Guide*, 58.

34. Blockson, *Hippocrene Guide*, 66, 70, 75–76.

35. Blockson, *Hippocrene Guide*, 66–72.

36. Frederick Douglass, *The Life and Times of Frederick Douglass* (New York: Library Classics, 1994), 710–711.

37. Douglass, *Life and Times* (Library Classics edition), 674.

38. Quarles, *Black Abolitionists*, 149.

39. Chadwick, *Traveling the Underground Railroad*, 182.

40. Jacqueline Tobin and Hettie Jones, *From Midnight to Dawn: The Last Tracks of the Underground Railroad* (New York: Doubleday, 2007), 23–26.

41. Switala, *Underground Railroad in Delaware, Maryland*, 76.

42. Switala, *Underground Railroad in Delaware, Maryland*, 77–78; Blockson, *Hippocrene Guide*, 26–27; and Still, *Underground Railroad*, 60.

43. Blockson, *Hippocrene Guide*, 28–29; Chadwick, *Traveling the Underground Railroad*, 250–252.

44. James A. McGowan, *Station Master on the Underground Railroad: The Life and Letters of Thomas Garrett* (Jefferson, NC: McFarland and Company, 2005), 121–123.

45. Smedley, *Chester County Underground Railroad*, 259–270; and William C. Kashatus, *Just Over the Line: Chester County and the Underground Railroad* (University Park, PA: Penn State Press, 2002), 49–67.

46. Some folklorists believe that quilt codes, done in geometric patterns and distinctive stitchings, were used to aid slaves in memorizing certain directives before their escape. Specific names, which functioned as metaphors in the code, were assigned to various quilt patterns. If a Monkey Wrench quilt pattern was being displayed, for example, slaves knew that they were to gather all the tools (belongings) they would need on an impending trip to the North. A Wagon Wheel pattern signified the method of transportation they would take. If a Tumbling Boxes pattern appeared, slaves knew that the moment of escape had arrived. However, it is unclear as to whether or not Harriet Tubman relied on quilt patterns to announce her arrival or to find a safe house on her journeys north. See Jacqueline L. Tobin and Raymond G. Dobard, *Hidden in Plain View: A Secret Story of Quilts and the Underground Railroad* (New York: Anchor, 2000), 69–71.

47. See William C. Kashatus, *In Pursuit of Freedom: Teaching the Underground Railroad* (Portsmouth, NH: Heinemann, 2005), 17–23.

48. For works on escape songs and spirituals, see Harold Courlander, *Negro Folk Music, U.S.A.* (New York: Dover, 1992); Miles M. Fisher,

Negro Slaves Songs in the United States (New York: Citadel, 1968); Samuel A. Floyd, Jr., *The Power of Black Music* (New York: Oxford University, 1995); and Arthur C. Jones, *Wade in the Water: The Wisdom of the Spirituals* (New York: Orbis, 1993).

49. Charles L. Blockson, "Escape from Slavery: The Underground Railroad," *National Geographic* (July 1984): 39; and Tobin and Dobard, *Hidden in Plain View*, 132.

50. Bradford, *Scenes from Life of Tubman*, 40.

51. African Methodist Episcopal Church of Auburn, New York, "Program of the Dedication of the Harriet Tubman Home, April 13, 1953," Harriet Tubman Pamphlets No. 1191m, Ithaca University Library, Ithaca, New York.

52. Kim Harris and Reggie Harris, *Music and the Underground Railroad* (Philadelphia: Ascension, 1984), 3–4; and Charles L. Blockson, *African Americans in Pennsylvania* (Baltimore: Black Classics, 1994), 12–13.

53. Humez, *Harriet Tubman*, 22.

54. Clinton, *Road to Freedom*, 85; and Larson, *Bound for the Promised Land*, 100.

55. Letter, Martha Coffin Wright to sisters, October 8, 1868, in Garrison Family Papers, Sophia Smith Collection, Smith College, Northampton, Massachusetts.

56. Margaret H. Bacon, *Valiant Friend: The Life of Lucretia Mott* (New York: Walker and Company, 1980), 186.

57. Horton, *Slavery and Making America*, 154.

58. Harriet Tubman, quoted in Bradford, *Scenes in the Life of Tubman*, 21–22.

Chapter 4

GOD SENDS HARRIET TO THOMAS GARRETT, 1854–1857

One late afternoon in mid-October 1856, Harriet arrived in Wilmington, Delaware, in need of funding for a rescue mission to the Eastern Shore. She went immediately to the office of Thomas Garrett, a white Quaker station master who also operated a hardware business in the town.

"God sent me to you, Thomas," said Harriet, dismissing the formality of a simple greeting. "He tells me you have money for me."

Amused by the request, Garrett jokingly asked: "Has God ever deceived thee?"

"No," she snapped.

"I have always been liberal with thee, Harriet, and wish to be of assistance," said the Quaker station master, stringing her along. "But I am not rich and cannot afford to give thee much."

Undeterred by the response, Harriet shot back: "God told me you've got money for me, and God *never* fools me!"

Realizing that she was getting upset, Garrett cut to the chase: "Well, then, how much does thee need?"

After reflecting a moment, Tubman said, "About 23 dollars."

The elderly Quaker shook his head in disbelief. Harriet's request was almost exactly the amount he had received from an antislavery society in Scotland for her specific use. He went to his cash box, retrieved the donation, and handed it to his visitor.

Smiling at her benefactor, Tubman took the cash, turned abruptly and marched out of the office.

Astonished by the incident, Garrett later confided to another abolitionist that "there was something remarkable" about Harriet. "Whether it [was] clairvoyance or the divine impression on her mind, I cannot tell," he admitted. "But I am certain she has a guide within herself other than the written word, for she never had any education."[1]

By most accounts, Tubman's behavior can be described as self-righteous, if not extremely presumptuous. But she viewed herself as being chosen by God for the special duty of a liberator. In fact, she admitted that she "felt like Moses," the Old Testament prophet, because "the Lord told me to go down South and bring up my brothers and sisters." When she expressed doubt about her abilities and suggested that the Lord "take somebody else," He replied: "It's you I want, Harriet Tubman."[2] With such a divine commission, Tubman was confident that her visions and actions—no matter how rude by 19th-century society's standards—were condoned by the Almighty. Thomas Garrett understood that. He shared Harriet's same passion for human freedom as well as a similar devotion to a higher law doctrine that opposed on religious grounds civil measures like the Fugitive Slave Law. Garrett struggled with a lifelong concern over slavery. Though he projected a genial disposition, the elderly Quaker could become abrasive when his antislavery convictions were challenged. Simply put: Garrett viewed slavery as a "concern," a Quaker term for a grievance that is so distressing to the individual that redressing it is pursued with an almost fanatical compulsion.

Unlike most other white abolitionists who saw slavery in abstract or constitutional terms, Garrett, like the slaves themselves, saw the institution in very personal terms. He, too, felt as if his own family had been violated by slavery when, in 1813, a slave catcher kidnapped a free black woman who worked on his parents' farm in Upper Darby, Pennsylvania. Garrett sped off to rescue her and on the way experienced a spiritual revelation about the utter sinfulness of slavery. Vowing to assist any fugitive, he joined the Pennsylvania Anti-Slavery Society

Thomas Garrett, ca. 1856. Garrett
(1789–1871) was a Quaker abolitionist who
gave Harriet Tubman financial assistance and
shelter on her rescue missions to Maryland's
Eastern Shore. (Courtesy of Chester County
Historical Society, West Chester, PA)

and dedicated himself to the Underground Railroad; it was a religious calling.[3] Accordingly, Garrett's behavior in regard to the Underground Railroad could also be interpreted by those who didn't know him as self-righteous.

In the 1820s, Garrett relocated to Wilmington, Delaware, where he opened a hardware store and established his home on Shipley Street, near Second Avenue, as a station on the Underground Railroad.[4] Harriet Tubman was a frequent guest at his home during the 1850s when she guided fugitives northward into southeastern Pennsylvania. He provided her at various times with shelter, food, clothing, shoes, and money. The two agents became close friends and co-conspirators, sharing an abiding faith that God would support them in their mission to rescue African Americans in bondage.[5]

Like Garrett, Tubman's religious faith was the inspiration for her role as an Underground Railroad agent. Throughout her life visions from her childhood head injury continued and she viewed them as divine premonitions. She often spoke of "consulting with God every day of her life," and she trusted that he would keep her safe.[6] Once, when she was guiding "several stout [fugitive] men" through the woods, God told Harriet to stop, leave the main path, and take a less traveled route. She obeyed and came to a stream of rapidly moving tidewater. God told her to go through it, in spite of the fact that it was early March and bitterly cold. Yet, Tubman did as she was told, "wading into the water up to her armpits." Not until she was safe on the opposite shore did the male fugitives follow.[7] Similar instances occurred on her rescue missions whenever Harriet was forced to make an important decision. She also believed that God led her to Garrett's station on several occasions, and that the Quaker agent would always provide for her needs. The two agents quickly became kindred spirits. In fact, Garrett compared Harriet's psychic ability to hear "the voice of God as spoken direct to her soul" to the Quakers' concept of an Inner Light, or a divine presence in each human being that allows them to do God's will on earth.[8] Because of their common emphasis on a mystical experience and a shared religious perspective, Tubman and the Quakers developed a mutual trust. However, not all Quakers were abolitionists and of those who were, certainly not all were Underground Railroad agents.

The Quaker belief in the equality of all human beings and the higher law principle compelled many individual Friends to become active abolitionists. Pennsylvania, in general, and Philadelphia, in particular, had a long history of abolitionism consonant with its Quaker founding in the 17th century.[9] As early as 1688, the Quakers of Germantown Meeting drafted the first antislavery petition in America. Acting on the Society of Friends' most fundamental belief of an Inner Light, or the presence of God in every human being, the Germantown Friends reasoned that if God manifested His presence in each individual, then, in His eyes, all humans were of equal value, regardless of race. Accordingly, they urged their Quaker brethren to "stand against the practice of bringing slaves to this country, or selling them against their own will."[10]

Not until 1759, however, did Philadelphia Yearly Meeting, the governing body of Friends in southeastern Pennsylvania, forbid members to continue any involvement in the slave trade.[11] Seventeen years later, in 1776, slaveholding was made a cause for disownment within the Religious Society of Friends.[12] Afterward, *individual* Friends shifted their antislavery crusade to the larger, non-Quaker society by appealing to the moral conscience of those who held slaves.

Only a minority of Quakers were abolitionists, and an even smaller percentage were Underground Railroad agents.[13] In fact, divisions over theology, social reform, and politics among Friends in Pennsylvania led to a schism between Philadelphia Yearly Meeting and more radical abolitionist members who established the Pennsylvania Yearly Meeting of Progressive Friends in 1853. Several members of this splinter group were active Underground Railroad agents on the Eastern Line, including Garrett, Elijah Pennypacker, and Lucretia Mott of Philadelphia.[14] The Progressive Friends dedicated themselves to the immediate abolition of slavery, a policy that was clearly articulated in their mission:

> In dealing with such a sin as slavery, we can adopt no halfway measures. The whole truth must be proclaimed, without concealment and without compromise. No Church, no Government, no Constitution, no Union, which requires us to support or sanction such a crime, can have any binding force upon our consciences. We seek not alone to prevent the *extension* of slavery, but to exterminate it immediately from every part of the land.[15]

Progressive Friends also believed that once freed, African Americans should enjoy the same liberties as whites. In one testimony after another, they decried the "cruel spirit of caste" which made the "complexion of even free Negroes a badge of social inferiority, exposing them to insult in the steamboat and railcar, and in all places of public resort, not even excepting the church."[16] "Ability" and "effort," they insisted, should supersede racial considerations.[17] Accordingly, Progressive Friends demanded equal educational opportunities and the full rights of citizenship for black people, including the ability to vote and hold office.[18]

Just as controversial was the Progressive Friends' involvement in the Underground Railroad. One member, Thomas Whitson, explained the group's justification for participating in this illegal movement shortly after the passage of the Fugitive Slave Law in 1850. "The popular notion that the government must be obeyed, whatever its requirements, is all wrong," he insisted. "Divine Law is superior to acts of Congress especially when it means destroying unjust measures."[19] Lucretia Mott, another Progressive Friend, echoed his sentiments. "Reformers ought to be satisfied to be destructives against unjust civil laws," she said. "If we are to be 'sharp threshing instruments having teeth' we should have some other name than 'reformers.'"[20]

Lucretia Mott, ca. 1865. A Progressive Quaker, Mott (1793–1880) was a leader of the early women's rights movement and a good friend to Harriet Tubman. (Courtesy of Chester County Historical Society, West Chester, PA)

The Progressive Friends built a meetinghouse at Longwood near Kennett, Chester County, which quickly became a center of radical abolitionism. On many occasions, the Longwood Meetinghouse was a gathering place for nationally famous leaders of the abolitionist movement, who traveled from all over the country to speak there. Abolitionists flocked to the site to attend open-air lectures by such distinguished abolitionists as Frederick Douglass, William Lloyd Garrison, Thomas Garrett, John Greenleaf Whittier, Sojourner Truth, and Susan B. Anthony.[21] The Progressive Friends also raised funds for antislavery societies across the North by conducting antislavery fairs.[22] At the same time, Progressive Friends never officially sponsored the Underground Railroad, realizing that to do so would imperil their own lives as well as those they were attempting to aid.[23]

Like the Presbyterian, Baptist, and Methodist Churches, which also divided over the issue of slavery, the Society of Friends was especially careful to distance itself from Progressive Friends and other members who participated in the illegal activities of the Underground Railroad.[24] Tubman, however, relied on these Quaker radicals for their support as conductors and station masters during the 11 years she was involved on the Underground Railroad.

Harriet was very trusting of the Quakers, which was unusual. Though she was highly intelligent, sagacious, and shrewd, she was also extremely cautious when dealing with people she didn't know. One of the ways she determined the credibility of an agent was to show them daguerreotypes of her friends. If the agent recognized the friend, he was all right. If not, she would quickly take leave of them.[25] Occasionally she preceded or followed the fugitives she was guiding between safe houses, especially if she was unfamiliar with the station master. In May 1856, for example, Harriet rescued four slaves from Norfolk, Virginia, and guided them to the home of Thomas Garrett. Garrett forwarded the runaways on to the station of a non-Quaker agent in Chester County, Pennsylvania. Tubman followed a day later, to insure their safety.[26]

Garrett was more than Harriet's friend and financier; he was, unwittingly, a recorder of her activities. Although the Wilmington Quaker destroyed all the letters he received from other Underground Railroad agents—to avoid incriminating himself as well as them—William Still and other abolitionists kept his correspondence, realizing its historical importance.[27] The letters trace Tubman's activities from the mid-1850s to 1860, the date of her last trip to the South.[28] Many of the specific details of Harriet's rescue missions can be attributed to his correspondence. In a letter dated December 29, 1854, for example, Garrett writes:

> We made arrangements last night, and sent away Harriet Tubman, with six men and one woman to Allen Agnew's, to be forwarded across the county to the city. Harriet and one of the men had worn the shoes off their feet, and I gave them two dollars to help fit them out, and directed a carriage to be hired at my expense, to take them out.[29]

The letter is very revealing, disclosing several vital facts: the number of fugitives accompanying Harriet (7); the time of her arrival at his station (the evening of December 28, 1854); the amount of money he gave Tubman ($2.00); the reason for the money (new shoes); the mode of transportation provided for the group (carriage); the station where they were sent (Allen Agnew, a Presbyterian farmer who lived in Kennett, just over the Mason-Dixon Line in Chester County, Pennsylvania); and the group's destination (Philadelphia).[30] Historians have also identified three of the male fugitives as Ben, Robert, and Henry Ross, three of Harriet's brothers.[31] This was one of Harriet's most famous rescue missions.

Tubman planned the rescue weeks in advance by dictating a letter to be sent to Jacob Jackson, a free black who resided in Dorchester County, Maryland. Trusting that Jackson would get word to her brothers, Harriet disclosed her intentions to rescue them but did it in code using biblical phrasing. In case the letter was intercepted by the civil authorities, she had it signed "William Henry Jackson," after Jacob's adopted son. Though white postal workers did discover the letter and questioned Jackson about its contents, he insisted that it was a case of mistaken identity since he had no idea who wrote it and that he had no brothers. As soon as he was released, however, Jackson got word of Harriet's plan to the Ross brothers.

The letter directed the three brothers to meet Harriet on Christmas Day at their parents' home in Caroline County. It was the most convenient time to schedule an escape since the enslaved brothers were permitted by their masters to spend the December holiday with family.

The decision to flee to the North must have been especially difficult for Henry Ross, whose wife went into labor just as he was about to leave for his parents' house. He delayed his departure so he could witness the birth of his child, but never told his wife of his intention. When the four siblings made their rendezvous at the Ross home, Harriet, realizing that her parents would be questioned about the escape, never made contact with her mother and had her father blindfolded so he could honestly re-port that he had not "seen" his daughter since she fled to the North five years earlier. The plan was carried out without incident, and in a timely fashion since all three brothers were about to be sold.[32]

To be sure, the contents of Garrett's letters were highly sensitive at a time when the federal government was attempting to shut down the operation of the Underground Railroad. At the same time, the letters confirm Tubman's association with Garrett and the nature of his op-eration as well as Harriet's reputation for guiding runaways to freedom. Other letters identify additional financiers of her rescue missions. On September 12, 1856, for example, Garrett sent a letter to sisters Eliza Wigham and Mary Edmundson of the Edinburgh Ladies Emancipation Society in Scotland. The sisters were Quakers and friends to some of the most noted American abolitionists, including William Lloyd Garrison, the editor of *The Liberator*, an antislavery newspaper; and Levi Coffin, a Quaker merchant from Cincinnati and the reputed informal president of the Underground Railroad's Western Line. They also raised and do-nated money for the clandestine network, channeling funds through Thomas Garrett.[33]

In the September 1856 letter, Garrett responded to an earlier inquiry the sisters made. They wanted to know if Garrett had any knowledge about the heroic deeds of a "colored woman" who traveled into the South at night and concealed herself in the woods to lead slaves out of bondage to freedom in the North. If he knew her, they wanted to send the woman some money—5 pounds sterling—to fund her rescue mis-sions. In his reply, Garrett admitted that he did not know for sure if the "colored woman" was Harriet Tubman, but he provided the following detailed description of her:

> She [Harriet] says she went to Canada some four months since, to pilot two fugitives, & was taken ill there, & is now just able to

travel again. She is to leave this day for Baltimore, to bring away
two slave children. When she returns, if successful, she will set
out for her sister & two children [that is her *sister's* two children],
on the coast of Maryland, near where her legal master now lives.
She is quite feeble, her voice much impaired from a cold taken last
winter, which I fear has permanently settled on her lungs.

   She told me, if she should be successful in getting the two from
Baltimore, & the sister & [the sister's] two children from the Eastern Shore, she would be satisfied to remain at home till her health
should be restored. The name of this noble woman is Harriet
Tubman, & she requests me to inform thee that the friends can send
the five pound sterling to aid her in her trustworthy calling.[34]

Pleased by Garrett's response, the Quaker sisters sent him the funds.
A few days later, Tubman arrived at his office and said, "Thomas, I am
here again, out of money, and with no shoes to my feet, and God has
sent me to you for what I need."

   "Harriet," replied Garrett, "I cannot find money enough to supply all
God's poor. I had five here last week and had to pay 8 dollars to clothe
and forward them."

   "Well, you've got enough for me to pay for a pair of shoes, and to pay
for my own and a friend's passage from Maryland to Philadelphia," she
countered.

   As usual, Garrett relented and gave her the funding for her trip.[35]
Taking the money from him, Harriet thanked him and returned to
Maryland, this time to rescue a young girl named Tilly.

   Tilly's fiancé pleaded with Harriet to rescue her from Baltimore and
bring her to Canada before she was sold into the Deep South. Garrett
noted "the trip was remarkable," and revealed Tubman's "great shrewdness." On the steamboat to Baltimore, Harriet purchased a ticket from
the captain indicating that she was a free black resident of Philadelphia. After retrieving the girl from Baltimore, Harriet, to avoid suspi-
cion, took another steamboat south to Seaford, Delaware. There, she
marched boldly into a hotel and ordered supper and lodging for her and
Tilly. The next morning as they were about to leave, a slave catcher attempted to arrest them.

But when Harriet presented the steamship captain's certificate, she and Tilly were allowed to pass.

Harriet then paid their passage on the railroad north to Camden, Delaware, where they received assistance from Underground Railroad agent William Brinkly, and arrived at Garrett's in a "private convey-ance." Garrett asked Harriet if she was frightened. "Not a bit," she re-plied. "I knew I would get off safe."[36]

In November 1856, Harriet returned to the South in another attempt to rescue her sister, Rachel. She made arrangements to meet her, but after waiting 10 days, Rachel decided that she could not leave with-out her children, Argerine and Ben, who were the property of another master. Harriet planned to return over the Christmas holidays when her sister would be reunited temporarily with her children.[37] Harriet would make two more attempts to rescue Rachel and her children dur-ing the next four years. Sadly, Rachel died before Harriet could rescue the entire family together and she would have to leave her sister's two orphaned children in slavery.[38]

When other freedom seekers learned that Tubman was on the Eastern Shore and that her sister was unwilling to leave without her children, they eagerly sought her services to take them north. This set the stage for one of the most popular rescue missions of Tubman's career. The fugitives on this journey were Josiah ("Joe") Bailey, his brother William ("Bill") Bailey, Peter Pennington, and Eliza Manokey. Joe had recently been purchased by William Hughlett, a prominent planter who owned some 40 slaves as well as thousands of acres along the Choptank River. Because Joe was a highly skilled slave, Hughlett had paid a high price for him, almost $2,000. But Hughlett also had a policy of reinforcing his authority as master by constant whippings. Joe witnessed other slaves being whipped and knew what had happened to them when they re-sisted. He pleaded with his owner to spare him, reminding his master that he had served him faithfully. "Hab you anything to complain of agin me?" he asked.

"No Joe," replied Hughlett, "I've no complaint to make of you. You're a good nigger, and you've always worked well; but the first lesson my niggers have to learn is that I am *master*, and they are not to resist or refuse to obey anything I tell 'em to do. So, the first thing they've got to do is be whipped; if they resist, they get it all the harder. But they got to give up at last and learn that I am master."

Joe took his whipping, but that night he decided it would be his last. Shortly after, he along with his brother Bill, Pennington, and Manokey escaped with Tubman.

When Hughlett discovered that his slave was missing he offered a reward of $1,500 for his capture. In addition, John Campbell Henry offered a reward of $300 for the capture of his slave, Bill Bailey, and Turpin Wright offered $800 for the capture of his chattel, Peter Pennington. Hughlett probably interpreted Joe's running away as a personal affront and, like Henry and Wright, pursued the runaway relentlessly. But Harriet's ingenuity as well as her knowledge of the terrain kept them safe from their pursuers.

Forced to move slowly and stay hidden for long periods of time, the trip from Maryland's Eastern Shore to Wilmington, which usually took four days, took almost two weeks. At one point, the group was forced to hide in holes used to store potatoes as the slave catchers passed within several feet of them. When Harriet reached the outskirts of Wilmington, she cautiously remained across the Christiana River waiting for Garrett's help. Hughlett, Henry, and Wright had arrived in Wilmington ahead of the group and posted signs offering rewards for their capture. Though the free black community tried to aid her by tearing down the signs, all the town's bridges were being watched. Garrett, who was under close surveillance himself, managed to hire three free blacks to load a wagon with bricks and cross one of the bridges posing as bricklayers. On their way across the next morning, they created a ruse by singing, laughing, and greeting the police who guarded the bridge. When they returned to Wilmington in the evening they did the same thing, only his time Harriet and her three runaways were hidden in the wagon's secret compartment. Garrett arranged to have another station master meet the group, and the next day Harriet led them safely to William Still's office in Philadelphia.

Joe was terrified throughout the trip. He knew that Hughlett would "whip to death" any slave who resisted him, and running away was the greatest act of resistance. When Harriet and the three fugitives reached the offices of the New York Anti-Slavery Society, Oliver Johnson, the secretary, recognized Joe immediately from an advertisement. Convinced that he was still in danger, Joe was ready to surrender to the authorities. At that point, Tubman gave him an ultimatum: go on to Canada or die by *her* hand. "From dat time Joe was silent," said Harriet. "He sang no more. He talked no more. He sat wid his head on his hand, and nobody could 'muse him or make him take any interest in anything."

Eventually Tubman led the group to the Niagara Falls Suspension bridge into Canada. Midway across, the fugitives were able to see the Promised Land on the other side. Harriet was anxious for all of them to look out the window to see the wonderful sight. They all came but Joe, who sat still with his head in his hands. "Joe, come look at de Falls," urged Harriet. "Joe, you fool, come see de Falls! It's your last chance." But Joe sat still and never raised his head. When Harriet was certain the group had crossed into Canada, she seized Joe and shaking him with all her might, cried, "Joe, you've shook de lion's paw! You're *free!*" Suddenly, the fugitive began sobbing with joy and sang aloud, "Glory to God and Jesus, too, one more Soul is safe."

Once Joe's feet touched the free soil of Canada, he was like a man possessed. His singing and shouting attracted a crowd so large that Harriet couldn't find him. After his brother and Pennington located Joe, the jubilant runaway eventually calmed down and said, "Oh, if I felt like dis down South, it would hab taken *nine* men to take me. Only one more journey for me now, and dat is to Hebben." To which Harriet replied "Well, you old fool, you might 'a looked at the Falls fust, and den gone to Hebben, after."[39]

Tubman's strong resolve was one of her most attractive characteristics for Garrett. He admired the fact that she refused to yield to runaways who became scared and pleaded to turn back or surrender to the authorities. He, too, was unyielding in his defense of the abolitionist cause. Found guilty of harboring a family of fugitive slaves in 1848, Garrett was heavily fined and warned by the court "not to meddle with slaves again." He grew defiant. "I have assisted over fourteen hundred runaways in twenty-five years on their way North," he told the federal marshal, "and I now consider the penalty imposed upon me as a license for the remainder of my life." To make matters worse, Garrett turned to the spectators who attended the trial and added, "If any of you know of any slave who needs assistance, send him to me, as I now publicly pledge myself to double my diligence and never neglect an opportunity to assist a slave in obtaining his freedom."[40] When slaveholders tried to intimidate him, Garrett met them placidly, never denying that he had aided fugitives. If they threatened him with weapons, he brushed them aside, commenting that "none but cowards resorted to such means." Once he was badly beaten and thrown off a train by a group of white Southerners. But the incident never discouraged his Underground Railroad activities. In fact, Garrett had a sense of humor about such confrontations. When an owner threatened to shoot him if he ever traveled South, the crusty old Quaker replied, "Well, I think I will be going that way before long and I will call upon thee."[41]

To be sure, Garrett was forthright about his activities, but not reckless. He never physically took up arms for the abolitionist cause and was probably surprised by the fact that Tubman carried a revolver and was not afraid to use it. Once a slave agreed to journey North, there was no turning back, and she threatened to shoot anyone who attempted to return to bondage.[42] Harriet once told of an expedition in which morale sank so low that one fugitive insisted on going back to the plantation.

Infuriated, Tubman pointed her revolver at his head and said: "You go on or die." The runaway became so frightened that there was not another word about returning to bondage, and several days later he crossed into Canada with the rest of the group.[43]

It was also Harriet's firm resolve that allowed her to achieve a long-time objective of freeing her own parents.

In March 1857, Harriet learned that her father, Benjamin Ross, was about to be arrested for helping eight slaves who escaped from jail in Dover, Delaware.[44] Ross had sheltered the six men and two women while they were in flight from Dorchester County, Maryland, and might have even provided them with pistols and knives for their protection. Once the group reached the Delaware border, they hired Thomas Otwell, a free black man living near Milford, to guide them to the next Underground Railroad station near Dover. Otwell was an experienced conductor who had once traveled with Harriet Tubman, but on this occasion he conspired with a slave catcher named Hollis to turn the runways in to the authorities for bounty money. Early on the morning of March 9, Otwell and the fugitives arrived in Dover where they met Hollis. Introducing the runaways as his "friends," Otwell turned the group over to Hollis, who was posing as another conductor. He took the fugitives to an unidentified building and led them into an upstairs room. When a gas lamp was lit, the group saw bars on the windows and realized they had been betrayed. No sooner did the sheriff arrive to lock them up than they staged a sensational escape. When the sheriff ran downstairs to his bedroom to get his pistols, the runaways followed in hot pursuit. One of the fugitives, Henry Prado, grabbed a hot andiron from the fireplace and held the lawman at bay while the others smashed a window for their escape. Prado then scattered hot coals over the floor of the bedroom so the sheriff couldn't follow.[45] The fugitives traveled north toward Wilmington and on their way they caught up with Otwell. Infuriated by his betrayal, they threatened to kill him until Otwell offered to guide them to a station where they could be assured of sanctuary. Although Garrett only gave refuge to two of the eight runaways, he was able to arrange for the safe passage of all of them over the Mason Dixon Line and into Chester County once he learned of their arrival in Wilmington.[46] Shortly after, Garrett wrote to William Still inquiring about Harriet Tubman's whereabouts:

Wilmington, 3rd mo., 27, 1857

Esteemed Friend, William Still:

I have been very anxious for some time past, to hear what has become of Harriet Tubman. The last I heard of her, she was in the State of New York, on her way to Canada with some friends, last fall. Hast thee seen or heard anything of her lately? It would be a sorrowful fact if such a hero as she should be lost from the Underground Railroad. If thee gets this in time, and knows anything respecting her, please drop me a line by mail tomorrow, and I will get it next morning, if not sooner.

Thomas Garrett[47]

After receiving the above letter, Still informed Garrett that Tubman was all right. "I was truly glad to learn that Harriet was still in good health and ready for action," Garrett wrote to Still, thanking him for the news. "But I think there will be more danger at present since there is so much excitement over the escape of the eight slaves."[48] The reason for Garrett's initial letter to Still may have been his concern for Ben Ross's safety. The Quaker station master might have learned about Ross's involvement in the escape of the Dover Eight and wanted to inform Harriet that her father could be in danger.

Though Ben Ross was a free man, life certainly had not been easy for him or his wife, Rit Green. He continued to work for his former owner's son, Dr. Anthony Thompson, who was "a wolf in sheep's clothing." According to Ross, Thompson claimed to be a "devout Methodist" but was actually a "rough man" who cheated him of his wages. He and his wife had also suffered the loss of several children who had been sold to the Deep South.[49] Though Ben had purchased his wife's freedom from Eliza Brodess for $20 two years earlier, the couple, both in their 80s, felt unsafe in an increasingly hostile environment.[50] If Harriet's father was arrested on the charge of assisting the Dover Eight, there would be nothing she could do. Thus, Ross's impending arrest provided the impetus for Harriet to act.

In early June, she approached Garrett and asked for money to finance her trip to the Eastern Shore, and he gave her 30 pounds sterling. With the money, Harriet purchased an "old horse, fitted out with a straw collar" and an old wooden wagon to transport her father to the North. When Harriet reached Ben, he "seemed delighted at the idea of going to a free country" like Canada, but he refused to leave without his wife, who lived on another plantation 20 miles away. After retrieving Rit, Harriet transported her parents the 80 miles to Wilmington in the old rig, keeping on the roads only at night. Once they arrived at Garrett's station, the Quaker agent gave Harriet and her parents the funds to travel by rail to St. Catharines, Ontario. There, at a community of former slaves, Harriet's parents were reunited with their five sons: Robert, James, Isaac, William Henry, Henry, and Benjamin. Fearing an arrest warrant, Ben and Rit changed their last name from Ross to Stewart, just as their sons had done when they relocated to Canada.[51] With her parents safely settled in Canada, Harriet made plans to return to the Eastern Shore to rescue her younger sister, Rachel, and her three children.

Although Tubman would return to the South just a few more times over the next three years, she had already sealed her reputation as a legend of the Underground Railroad. Her indefatigable efforts at leading mass escapes gained her national and international fame, and abolitionists in the United States, Scotland, and England heralded her achievements and donated money to her cause.[52] Tubman's righteous self-determination inspired others who shared her disdain of slavery.

NOTES

1. Letter, Thomas Garrett to Eliza Wigham, Wilmington, Delaware: October 24, 1856, quoted in James A. McGowan, *Station Master on the Underground Railroad: The Life and Letters of Thomas Garrett* (Jefferson, NC: McFarland and Company, 2005), 171–172.

2. Rosa Belle Holt, "A Heroine in Ebony," *Chautauquan* 23 (July 1886): 461.

3. McGowan, *Station Master*, 31–37.

4. McGowan, *Station Master*, 43.

5. McGowan, *Station Master*, 98–114.

6. Harriet Tubman, quoted in Catherine Clinton, *Harriet Tubman: The Road to Freedom* (New York: Little, Brown, 2004), 91.

7. McGowan, *Station Master*, 100.

8. Garrett, quoted in McGowan, *Station Master*, 100.

9. Charles L. Blockson, "Escape from Slavery: The Underground Railroad," *National Geographic Magazine* 166, no. 1 (July 1984): 23; and William J. Switala, *Underground Railroad in Pennsylvania* (Mechanicsburg, PA: Stackpole Books, 2001), 141.

10. Francis Daniel Pastorius, "Germantown Protest, 1688," quoted in Thomas E. Drake, *Quakers and Slavery in America* (New Haven: Yale University Press, 1950), 34; and Donna McDaniel and Vanessa Julye, *Fit for Freedom, Not for Friendship: Quakers, African Americans, and the Myth of Racial Justice* (Philadelphia: Quaker Press, 2009), 15–22.

11. Jean Soderlund, *Quakers and Slavery: A Divided Spirit* (Princeton, NJ: Princeton University Press, 1985), 90–92; and Gary B. Nash and Jean R. Soderlund, *Freedom by Degrees: Emancipation in Pennsylvania and Its Aftermath* (New York: Oxford University Press, 1991), 4–9.

12. Philadelphia Yearly Meeting Minutes: 1776; Jack Marietta, *The Reformation of American Quakerism, 1748–1783* (Philadelphia: University of Pennsylvania Press, 1984); and McDaniel & Julye, *Fit for Freedom*, 29–42.

13. William Still, in an 1858 interview of fugitive Asbury Irwin, identifies at least one Quaker—Michael Newbold of Kent County, Maryland—as a slaveholder. Newbold's "drinking, horse racing and abuse of his slaves as well as his wife" suggest that he was disowned by the Society of Friends. Still casts doubt on Asbury's accusation that his former owner was a Quaker, however, writing that it was "too shocking to morality and damaging to humanity" to believe. See William Still, *Underground Railroad* (1872; reprinted Chicago: Johnson Publishing, 1970), 506–507. In addition, William C. Kashatus identifies the various degrees of involvement southeastern Pennsylvania's Quakers had in the abolitionist movement as well as on the Underground Railroad. See William C. Kashatus, *Just Over the Line: Chester County and the Underground Railroad* (University Park, PA: Penn State Press, 2002), 35–67.

14. Pennsylvania Yearly Meeting of Progressive Friends, *Proceedings* (1853): 5, in the collections of the Chester County Historical Society, West Chester, PA. For a more detailed account of the Progressive Friends, see Albert J. Wahl, "The Congregational or Progressive Friends in the Pre-Civil War Reform Movement" (PhD dissertation, Temple University, 1951).

15. Pennsylvania Yearly Meeting of Progressive Friends (hereafter PYMPF), *Proceedings* (1853), 43–44. Chester County Historical Society, West Chester, Pennsylvania.

16. "*Caste*," PYMPF, *Proceedings* (1858), 35.

17. "Complexional Distinctions," PYMPF, *Proceedings* (1863), 16.

18. "Complexional Distinctions," PYMPF, *Proceedings* (1863), 16; and "Caste," PYMPF, *Proceedings* (1858), 35.

19. Thomas Whitson, quoted in *Pennsylvania Freeman*: November 4, 1853.

20. Lucretia Mott to Martha Wright, Chelten Hills, Pennsylvania: December 5, 1861. Friends Historical Library, Swarthmore College, Swarthmore, Pennsylvania.

21. Kashatus, *Just Over the Line*, 64.

22. *Pennsylvania Freeman*: February 23, March 30, May 4, 1854.

23. William Still, *Underground Railroad*, 712; and Albert J. Wahl, "The Congregational or Progressive Friends in the Pre-Civil War Reform Movement" (PhD dissertation, Temple University, 1951), 292.

24. See Ryan P. Jordan, *Slavery and the Meetinghouse: The Quakers and the Abolitionist Dilemma, 1820–1865* (Bloomington: Indiana University, 2007), 81–103; McDaniel & Julye, *Fit for Freedom*, 96–106; William W. Sweet, *The Story of Religion in America* (New York: Harper & Row, 1930), 170–180; David Christy, *Pulpit Politics, or Ecclesiastical Legislation on Slavery in Its Disturbing Influences on the American Union* (New York: Farran and McLean, 1862); and Switala, *Underground Railroad in Pennsylvania*, 165–175.

25. Sarah H. Bradford, *Scenes in the Life of Harriet Tubman* (Auburn, NY: W. J. Moses, 1869), 81.

26. Letter, Thomas Garrett to J. Miller McKim and William Still, Wilmington, Delaware: May 11, 1856, in McGowan, *Station Master*, 141.

27. McGowan, *Station Master*, 134.

28. Garrett's biographer James A. McGowan contends that the first recorded instance in which the Quaker station master speaks of Tubman is in a December 29, 1854, letter to J. Miller McKim of the Pennsylvania Anti-Slavery Society. The tone of the letter suggests that Garrett had known her for some time. See McGowan, *Station Master*, 138. Garrett's last communication dealing with Tubman as an Underground Railroad agent is a December 1, 1860 letter to William Still (see McGowan, *Station Master*, 152–153). Other letters disclosing Tubman's Underground Railroad activities were preserved by Eliza Wigham and Mary Edmundson, sisters who raised money for Tubman's rescue missions as members of the Edinburgh [Scotland] Ladies Emancipation Society.

29. Letter, Thomas Garrett to J. Miller McKim, Wilmington, DE: December 29, 1854, quoted in McGowan, *Station Master*, 138.

30. Allen Agnew's station at Kennett was one of several options Garrett had in Chester County, Pennsylvania, where he worked with a diverse group of agents, free black and white, male and female, Quaker and non-Quaker. See Kashatus, *Just Over the Line*, 21, 94–96.

31. Still, *Underground Railroad*, 305–307; Bradford, *Scenes in the Life of Tubman*, 57–58; Kate Clifford Larson, *Bound for the Promised Land: Harriet Tubman, Portrait of an American Hero* (New York: Ballantine Books, 2004), 93–94; and Fergus M. Bordewich, *Bound for Canaan: The Underground Railroad and the War for the Soul of America* (New York: Amistad, 2005), 374–375.

32. Clinton, *Road to Freedom*, 96–97.

33. McGowan, *Station Master*, 162.

34. Letter, Thomas Garrett to Eliza Wigham, Wilmington, Delaware: September 12, 1856, in McGowan, *Station Master*, 169–170. Unfortunately, Harriet was unable to rescue her sister on that particular trip. The sister in question was Rachel, the youngest of her four female siblings.

35. McGowan, *Station Master*, 102.

36. Letter, Thomas Garrett to Eliza Wigham: October 24, 1856, in McGowan, *Station Master*, 171–172.

37. Larson, *Bound for the Promised Land*, 133.

38. Humez, *Harriet Tubman*, 42, 230–231; and Ednah Dow Cheyney, "Moses," *Freedmen's Record* 1 (March 1865): 35–36.

39. Bradford, *Scenes in the Life of Tubman*, 27–35; and Larson, *Bound for the Promised Land*, 133–136.

40. Garrett quoted in McGowan, *Station Master*, 64–65.

41. Smedley, *Underground Railroad in Chester County*, 241.

42. Clinton, *Road to Freedom*, 90–91.

43. Conrad, *Tubman Biography*, 14.

44. Bradford, *Scenes in the Life of Tubman*, 48.

45. Letter, Thomas Garrett to Samuel Rhoads, Wilmington, Delaware: March 1857 in McGowan, *Station Master*, 109.

46. *Delaware Recorder* (Wilmington, Delaware): April 3, 1857.

47. Letter, Thomas Garrett to William Still, Wilmington, Delaware: March 27, 1857, quoted in McGowan, *Station Master*, 110.

48. Letter, Thomas Garrett to William Still, Wilmington, Delaware: March 1857, quoted in McGowan, *Station Master*, 143.

49. Still, *Underground Railroad*, 411.

50. Larson, *Bound for the Promised Land*, 119.

51. Letter, Thomas Garrett to Mary Edmondson, Wilmington, Delaware: August 11, 1857, in McGowan, *Station Master*, 182–183; and Larson, *Bound for the Promised Land*, 143–144.

52. Bradford, *Scenes in the Life of Tubman*, 52.

Chapter 5

INSPIRED BY JOHN BROWN, 1858–1860

During the spring of 1858, Harriet experienced a recurring dream in which she found herself in "a wilderness of rocks and bushes." Suddenly a "big snake raised his head from behind a rock" and transformed "into the head of an old man with a long white beard." Captivated by the vision, Tubman moved closer. The wizened figure returned her gaze in a "wishful" manner, but just as he was about to speak, a crowd of men rushed in and struck him down.[1]

Harriet interpreted the dream as a sign of some sort, though the meaning was unclear until April 7 when she was introduced to John Brown, a radical abolitionist who advocated the use of violence to destroy slavery in the United States.

Brown, who was in his late 50s and also sported a long white beard, had just arrived in the Canadian town of St. Catharines where he had guided a group of 11 slaves to freedom. To his surprise, he discovered that Tubman was there as well. When introduced to each other, Brown, in a strange ritualistic greeting, shook her hand three times, saying: "The first I see is General Tubman, the second is General Tubman, and the third is General Tubman." It was an expression of his great admiration for Tubman's bravery in guiding mass escapes on the Underground Railroad.[2]

Harriet was impressed by the radical abolitionist. She knew of his bloody massacre of proslavery forces in Kansas two years earlier as well as his remarkable rescue of 11 slaves from Missouri, at gunpoint, the previous winter. Now they were face to face.

When Brown outlined his elaborate plot to stage a slave uprising that might lead to a full-scale war, Harriet was extremely supportive of such direct action and she even made several thoughtful suggestions. Now her dream was clear: the "wishful face" was that of John Brown and he had wanted to tell her of his plan to end slavery. Brown and Tubman spent very little time together after their initial meeting. But from that point on they shared a strong emotional and intellectual bond.[3]

Tubman had always viewed slavery as a sin, but not until she met Brown did she consider it a state of war. Although she had not supported physical violence against whites to that time, she, like Brown, disdained abolitionists who were unwilling to use direct action. If slavery could be destroyed through armed resistance, Harriet was willing to join Brown's insurrection, a plan he had been cultivating for some time.[4]

John Brown, a native of New England, spent most of his life in Ohio. A tanner by trade, he failed in several business ventures. He also circulated among abolitionists and endeared himself to African Americans by living in black neighborhoods, adopting a black child and raising him along with his other four sons. Initially, Brown's antislavery activities were limited to conducting slaves on the Underground Railroad, but he eventually adopted the belief that slavery could only be ended when the "land was purged with blood."[5] To that end, he formed, in 1850, the "United States League of Gileadites," a group of black men and women who pledged to arm themselves and kill anyone seeking to kidnap or arrest any African American, free or slave. He also concocted a scheme to establish a guerilla base in the Virginia mountains from which he would launch raids on surrounding plantations to free the slaves and pass them on to freedom in the North.[6]

In 1855, Brown and his five sons relocated to Kansas, a territory that had recently been opened for the possible expansion of slavery by Congress. According to the Kansas-Nebraska Act, the issue would be decided by the popular sovereignty of those who settled there. Although

the vast majority of Kansas settlers were independent farmers inter-
ested in finding good land, pro- and antislavery minorities turned the
territory into a bloody battleground of sectional politics. When the
election of the first territorial legislature was finally held, throngs of
proslavery advocates from Missouri crossed the border and stuffed the
ballot boxes. Although there were only 2,900 registered voters living in
Kansas, over 6,000 ballots were cast. The proslavery border ruffians, as
they were called, had stolen the election for the proslavery settlers. In
retaliation, the antislavery Free Soilers formed their own government.
As a result, Kansas had both a proslavery territorial legislature in Le-
compton and an antislavery government in Topeka.

The new proslavery government immediately set out to crush its
opposition and make Kansas a slave territory. In 1856, when proslavery
forces sacked the "free state" town of Lawrence, Brown sought revenge
by leading an assault on a proslavery settlement at Pottawatomie Creek,
killing five reputed proslavery settlers. The act provoked more vigilantism from both sides. Armed bands roamed the countryside burning towns and killing innocent victims. Dubbed by the newspapers as
"Bleeding Kansas," vigilantism became so common that John Brown
and his followers became merely one of several murderous bands who
were never arrested, never brought to trial, and never stopped from
committing further violence. Still, Brown justified the murders as "obedience to the will of a just God," and he became a hero among Northern
extremists.[7]

Brown's plans for a bloody insurrection against the South became
solidified in 1857 after the *Dred Scott* decision. Scott, a Missouri slave,
had been taken by his owner, army surgeon John Emerson, to live in the
free state of Illinois and, later, to Minnesota Territory, where slavery was
also illegal. Scott married a female slave while in Minnesota and the
couple's daughter was also born there. Although Scott and his family
eventually returned to Missouri, the slave, in 1846, sued for his and his
family's freedom, insisting that residence on free soil made them free. It
took 11 years for the case to reach the Supreme Court, and when it did,
the ruling went against Scott and his family.

On March 6, 1857, Chief Justice Roger B. Taney, a 79-year-old
Maryland slaveholder, read the majority opinion in one of the Supreme
Court's most controversial rulings. Declaring the Missouri Compromise

John Brown. Reproduction
of a daguerreotype taken by
Martin M. Lawrence ca. May
1859. A radical abolitionist,
Brown (1800–1859) enlisted
Tubman to help plan his
October 1859 insurrection at
Harpers Ferry. (Courtesy of
the Library of Congress)

unconstitutional, Taney contended that the federal government had
no right to interfere with the free movement of property throughout
the territories. In other words, a slaveholder could take his slaves any-
where in the Union, including free states, without losing title to them.
As a result, Taney dismissed the Dred Scott case on the grounds that
Scott was still a slave because he returned to Missouri before filing suit
and only United States citizens could bring suits before federal courts.
Taney's ruling carried the Supreme Court by a 7-2 decision. The five
Southern members concurred, as did one Northern justice, Robert C.
Grier, who was pressured by newly elected President James Buchanan,
a fellow Pennsylvanian, to support the majority. Two of the three other
Northerners vigorously dissented, and the last voiced other objections.
Clearly, the ruling was a sectional decision, and it further divided the
nation along sectional lines.[8]

　　Infuriated by the law, Brown, like most Northern abolitionists, believed that anger among slaves was so great that a general uprising

needed only a spark to be ignited. As a result, he traveled east raising money for his wild scheme to lead a slave insurrection, recruiting soldiers and conducting meetings with abolitionists. During the early months of 1858, Brown traveled to Boston to meet with six prominent abolitionists: Gerritt Smith, George L. Stearns, Franklin B. Sanborn, Thomas W. Higginson, Theodore Parker, and Samuel G. Howe. At the meeting, he revealed an elaborate plan to invade the South, foment a general slave rebellion, and establish a free state for former slaves under a new constitution. Although they agreed to finance the operation, the six men, later called the Secret Six, were unwilling to participate in the assault.[9] Other prominent abolitionists responded the same way when approached by Brown. Their reaction was understandable. Mounting frustration over the failure of Congress and the courts to achieve peaceful emancipation made many abolitionists receptive to a more militant approach. Some even promoted direct action in their speeches and writings. The famous black orator Frederick Douglass, for example, condemned the Fugitive Slave Law of 1850 by suggesting that "a dozen or more dead kidnappers carried down South would cool the ardor of Southern gentlemen, and keep their rapacity in check."[10] Douglass continued his militant rhetoric throughout the 1850s, but after Brown tried to enlist him in his army the great orator was hesitant to offer anything but moral support.[11] Tubman was more supportive.

On April 7, 1858, Brown, who had come to St. Catharines to recruit fugitive slaves for his army, met with Harriet, then living in a rented house on North Street. Since there are no eyewitness accounts of the meeting, it's not certain what Brown told her of his plans. However, Tubman's familiarity with former slaves living in Canada could be useful in recruiting potential insurgents. In addition, her knowledge of support networks and resources in the border states of Pennsylvania, Maryland, and Delaware could prove to be invaluable to him as he refined his plans for an invasion of the South.[12] Whatever the case might have been, Brown was pleased with their meeting as he wrote to his son the following day informing him that "I am succeeding to all appearance beyond my expectations." "Harriet Tubman took on his whole team at once," Brown added. "He [Harriet] is the most of a man, naturally, I ever met with."[13]

Brown's use of the masculine pronoun in describing Harriet was actually a sign of respect. He categorized armed resistance and martial
pursuits in the man's sphere, not the woman's. Because he was so impressed with Tubman's courage in guiding slaves out of bondage at great
personal risk, Brown not only gave her the title "General," but also
honored her with the masculine pronoun. In addition, Brown, who flat-
tered himself as similar to an Old Testament patriarch, may have condemned the second-class citizenship of black men, but had no difficulty
in embracing the subservient status of women.[14] Tubman reciprocated
by stumping across New England raising funds for Brown's campaign
over the next year. It is also believed that she encouraged Brown to
conduct his invasion on July 4, 1858, believing that the anniversary of
American independence would be ideal to commemorate by freeing
the slaves.[15] Instead, Brown chose to strike in mid-May and conducted
a secret convention of his supporters in Chatham, Canada, in late April
to solidify his plans.[16] At that meeting, Brown gathered his band of
12 co-conspirators and 34 African American recruits and revealed that
the invasion would start by taking control of the federal arsenal at
Harpers Ferry in northwestern Virginia. From there, his guerilla force
would arm the slaves who, in turn, would rise up and carry out an armed
rebellion across the South. But when word of his intentions leaked to
the government, he put his plans on hold.[17]

Tubman and Brown met once more in late May. The meeting took
place in Boston, where Harriet had come to raise funds for her next
Underground Railroad rescue. Brown may have informed her of a new
date for the invasion, though this is only conjecture. Harriet also met
Thomas Wentworth Higginson, a Unitarian minister who was a member of Brown's Secret Six and one of his biggest financial supporters.
Shortly after, Higginson wrote a letter to his mother testifying to the
high esteem in which he held Tubman:

We have had the greatest heroine of the age here, Harriet Tubman. She is a black woman and fugitive slave, who has been back
[to the South] eight times and [rescued] in all sixty slaves, including her own family. Her tales of adventure are beyond anything
in fiction and her generalship is extraordinary. I have known of

her for some time and mentioned in speeches once or twice. The slaves call her "Moses." She has a reward of $12,000 offered for her in Maryland and will probably be burned alive whenever she is caught, which she probably will be. She has been in the habit of working in hotels all summer, saving up money for this crusade in the winter.[18]

No doubt Higginson was impressed just as much by Tubman's reputation as her presence. The minister who agreed to finance Brown—but not to participate in his insurrection—appears to have been drawn to individuals who displayed great courage of conviction. But he was also too cautious to be more than an admirer and financier of their causes, lest he, too, "be caught" and "burned alive" like Tubman.

Repeated postponements and poor communication prevented Brown from launching his assault for another year. It also prevented him from locating Harriet, who was busy giving talks to abolitionist audiences and tending to her parents and other relatives.[19] As a result, Tubman did not play any significant role on the day of the invasion, but she did have a premonition that he was in trouble. On October 16, 1859—the day of Brown's raid at Harpers Ferry—Harriet was visiting friends in New York and told her hostess that "something was wrong, but she could not tell what." Later that evening she came to the conclusion that "it must be Captain Brown" and told her friend that they would "soon hear bad news from him."[20] The next day's newspapers confirmed her worst fears.

During the previous night, Brown set out for Harpers Ferry with 21 followers and a wagon full of supplies. Leaving three men behind to guard their base camp—a nearby farm—Brown's guerillas slipped into town and easily seized control of the arsenal. To his surprise, however, none of the local slaves would join his revolt. Most were afraid that Brown would be unsuccessful and did not want to risk their lives for a fanatic. Even more incredible, Brown had made no provision for escape. Within three days, federal troops under the command of Colonel Robert E. Lee captured Brown and 6 of his men. Another 10 of his followers were killed in the ambush. Brown and his surviving men were convicted of treason, conspiracy, and first-degree murder. All the charges carried the death penalty. Throughout his trial, the radical abolitionist spoke passionately against slavery and accepted his death sentence with the calm resignation of a martyr.[21] Holding a bible in his right hand, Brown told the court:

> I had early learned to do unto others as I would do unto myself. It teaches me further to remember them that are in bonds, as bound with them. I endeavored to act up to that instruction . . .
>
> Now if it is deemed necessary that I should forfeit my life for the furtherance of the ends of justice, and mingle my blood with the blood of millions in this slave country whose rights are disregarded by wicked, cruel, and unjust enactments, I say let it be done.[22]

On December 1, 1859, Harriet confided to a close friend that when she thought of John Brown and "how he gave up his life for our people," it was clear to her that he "wasn't a mortal man," but that there "was God in him." "When I think of all the groans on the plantations, and remember that God is a prayer-hearing God," she added, "I feel that his time is drawing near."

"Then you think that God's time for Captain Brown is near?" asked the friend.

"God's time is always near," replied Harriet.[23]

At 11:30 A.M. the following morning, the state of Virginia hanged John Brown.

News of Brown's raid electrified the North, where he immediately became a martyr for abolitionism. Public rites of mourning were conducted for him. Church bells tolled, buildings were draped in black, prayer meetings were held, and ministers extolled Brown's virtue in their sermons. On the other hand, Brown's failed insurrection outraged the white South because it struck at their greatest fear—slave rebellion. Southerners saw the raid as evidence that Northern abolitionists were bent on provoking slave revolts. Their fears were confirmed when documents captured at Harpers Ferry revealed that Brown had the financial support of the Secret Six, some of the wealthiest abolitionists in the North. People in both regions questioned Brown's sanity, and even those who admired him questioned his methods. But Tubman never wavered in her belief that Brown was "Christ-like" in that he "gave up his life for our people."[24] His example inspired her to be even more proactive on the Underground Railroad than she had been in the past and to free whatever family member remained in bondage.

Between 1857 and 1859, Harriet's attentions had been divided between her antislavery activities and a growing concern for her parents. Though she had relocated them to Canada, Ben and Rit, now in their early 80s, had difficulty adjusting to the harsh Canadian winters. Harriet spent two years searching for a new home and, in the spring of 1859, purchased a small piece of property on the outskirts of Auburn, New York, for them.

Auburn, the seat of Cayuga County in upstate New York, was a predominantly white farming community. Its population never exceeded five thousand, with only a smattering of free black residents. But the town also had a strong abolitionist element that included U.S. Senator William H. Seward. Seward was one of Auburn's Underground Railroad operators and had become a good friend to Harriet.[25] Desirous of helping her, the senator agreed to sell the house and the adjoining seven acres for just $1,200. It was quite a bargain. Originally a farm, the property consisted of a house, a barn, several outbuildings, and tillable land. It would provide ample space for Harriet, her parents, and any other family members who needed a home. Seward also offered generous terms of payment. Harriet made an initial payment of $25, and agreed to make quarterly payments of $10 with interest.[26] Although Auburn was a hotbed of antislavery activism, Seward was taking a significant risk by selling the property to her. It was illegal to sell land to a woman, and especially to a fugitive slave. If knowledge of the sale was made known to Congress, his political career would be over and he would be incarcerated. Tubman was also taking a huge risk. By returning to the United States she and her family were at risk of being returned to the South under the Fugitive Slave Law.[27] But it was a risk she felt she had to take to keep her family together.

Shortly after purchasing the Auburn property, Harriet returned to Maryland to rescue an eight-year-old mulatto girl named Margaret. In her adulthood, the girl was identified at various times as "Margaret Tubman" and as "Margaret Stewart." According to her reminiscences, written in later life, she was Harriet Tubman's niece and was kidnapped by her aunt from her parents and a twin brother who resided on the Eastern Shore. Margaret also claimed that her father, who was allegedly

Harriet's brother, was a free man and the head of a prosperous household. Tubman secreted the child north by steamboat. On the journey, Margaret was so taken with her aunt that she "forgot to weep over her separation from her twin brother and her mother."[28]

The details of the rescue mission as well as the relationship between Harriet and the child are not clear. There is confusion about the identity of Margaret's parents as well as Harriet's motive for taking the child if she were, in fact, the daughter of her brother, who was a free black man and the head of a prosperous household. For example, there is no record of a free black brother in the Ross family. If one did exist, why would Harriet, who spent so many years trying to reunite her own family, kidnap a niece who was living with a free household? Some historians speculate that Margaret may have been Tubman's daughter since the two shared a physical resemblance and an unusually strong bond of affection for each other. In addition, Harriet, who was in her forties, was beginning to realize that she would never have children and longed to have a daughter of her own. Since Margaret was born in 1850, months after Harriet escaped from slavery, Tubman may had fled because she was pregnant and did not want her child to be born into bondage. If she gave birth in flight, Harriet may have left the baby in the care of a free black family with an infant son who could have passed Margaret off as his twin.[29] On the other hand, Harriet herself denied that she gave birth to any children when, in 1894, she appeared at the Cayuga County (New York) Courthouse to apply for a pension for her wartime service. Why would she lie about her own child if the major priority in her own life was her family?[30] The truth will probably never be known. What is certain is that Harriet adopted Margaret and entrusted her to Frances Seward, William Seward's wife. Frances raised the little girl in her own household at Auburn, teaching her to read, write, and sew. She also made sure that Margaret paid regular visits to Harriet. By adolescence, Margaret had acquired the proper etiquette of a lady; something in which Harriett took great pride.[31]

In April 1860, Harriet was visiting a cousin in Troy, New York, en route to an abolitionist meeting in Boston. While walking the streets of Troy, she heard a commotion at the Mutual Bank Building where a crowd had gathered. William Henry, a black grocer and member of the Troy Vigilance Committee, explained the reason for the ruckus. Pointing to the second story of the building, he shouted: "There's a fugitive

slave in that office!" The Bank Building housed the office of U.S. magistrate Miles Beach, who had just ruled that Charles Nalle, a captured
runaway, be returned to slavery in Virginia. Pushing through the mob,
Harriet caused a disturbance by blocking the stairway to the second
floor office. Meanwhile, Nalle's rescuers managed to free him and take
him down to the Hudson River where he boarded a skiff. Though Nalle
was recaptured at West Troy on the other side of the river, Harriet and
the other abolitionists arrived on ferry, stormed the building where he
was held, and guided him to safety in the town of Niskayuna, just outside of Schenectady. Nalle remained in hiding there until 51 abolitionists purchased his freedom for $650.[32]

The same spring, Harriet began a new career as speaker at antebellum reform gatherings. In May of that year, she appeared before the New
England Anti-Slavery Society Conference and, the following month,
she delivered a speech on women's suffrage before a women's rights
session in Boston. Her stature as an Underground Railroad agent had
elevated Harriet to the same renown as such distinguished orators as
Wendell Phillips and William Lloyd Garrison. But that status came at
a price.

Proslavery advocates began to threaten Tubman's safety. One of her
critics was John Bell Robinson of Philadelphia, who had read about
her appearance before the Boston abolitionist convention that spring.
"What could be more insulting after having lost over $50,000 worth of
property by that deluded negress, than for a large congregation of whites
and well educated people of Boston to endorse such an imposition on
the Constitutional rights of the slave States?" he asked. Certainly, white
Bostonians were too intelligent to be fooled by an uneducated "deluded
negress" like Tubman.

Robinson also condemned Harriet's mission to rescue her elderly
parents from the South. "Now there are no old people of any color more
caressed and better taken care of than the old worn-out slaves of the
South," he insisted, painting slavery as a benevolent welfare system
shouldered by whites for the benefit of blacks. "Those old slaves had
earned their living while young, and a home for themselves when past
labor, and had sat down at ease around the plentiful board of their master whose duty it was to support them through old age, and see them
well taken care of in sickness, and when dead to give them a respect-
able burying." Robinson added that Tubman's parents would have been

better off remaining in the South where the laws compelled their owner to "give them support righteously due them for the balance of their days" instead of coming North where they will have "no rich white man or woman to call them 'Uncle Tom, and Aunt Lotta.'" Robinson concluded his invective by condemning Tubman's "diabolical" and "fiendish" ways by secreting her parents off to the North. "She should receive life imprisonment for her crime," he said. "It was cruel an act as ever was performed by a child toward parents."[33]

Slaveholders in the border states posed a greater danger to Tubman. Frustrated with their loss of control over their human property, they issued stiffer fines against anyone found guilty of aiding fugitives. Harriet became their primary target as they placed bounties on her ranging from $12,000 to $40,000.[34] Some were so brazen as to debate publicly the "cruel devices by which she would be tortured and put to death."[35] Harriet's abolitionist friends pleaded with her to suspend her Underground Railroad activities for fear of her safety. Reluctantly she agreed after making one final journey to the Maryland's Eastern Shore.[36]

In late November 1860, Harriet set out for Dorchester County, Maryland, intending to bring her sister Rachel and her two children out of slavery. But when she arrived on the Eastern Shore she learned that Rachel had died and that the children could only be rescued if she paid a $30 bribe. Harriet had no money and was opposed by principle to paying for the freedom of a slave, even if they were members of her own family.[37] Sadly, she redirected her mission to rescue seven other slaves, including a couple with twin babies. As she proceeded north up the Delmarva Peninsula, the group was caught in a blinding rainstorm. Harriet attempted to seek refuge with one of the station masters who had assisted her in the past. But as they entered the town the infants began to cry uncontrollably, threatening to expose the entire group. Fearing for their safety, Harriet drugged the babies with opium to quiet them.

When they reached the safe house, she hid the fugitives in back and went around to the front door. Using the ritual knock that signaled her arrival, Harriet waited patiently for someone to answer. But no one came to the door.

After several moments, a window opened and a man stuck his head out. "Who are you?" he asked gruffly. "What do you want?" This was not the welcome that Harriet had received in the past.

When Harriet inquired about the station master, she was told that he was run out of town for "harboring niggers."

Realizing the danger she had created for her charges, Harriet quickly retreated and hurried the fugitives to a swamp outside of town. Because of the tall grass and the putrid odor, the swamp provided an ideal cover; no one would suspect it as a hiding place. Wading into the swamp, Harriet carried the drugged twins in a basket as the other fugitives followed. She ordered them to lie down in the tall, wet grass. Though they were all cold, tired, and hungry, Tubman refused to leave for supplies, knowing that the man she just encountered had given notice to the townspeople of her arrival.

At dusk, Harriet was awakened by the voice of a Quaker who appeared to be talking to himself. "My wagon stands in the barn-yard of the next farm across the way," he was saying as he walked slowly on the edge of the swamp. "The horse is in the stable and the harness hangs on a nail." She recognized him as the station master who had been driven out of town by his proslavery neighbors. Not waiting for a response, the Quaker simply continued on his path quietly repeating the same words.

When night fell, Harriet guided the group to the barn and to her delight discovered not only a wagon, but one that was full of provisions for the fugitives on her rescue mission.[38] She drove the wagon to Wilmington where she stayed with Thomas Garrett. On December 1, the Quaker station master wrote to William Still to let him know that Harriet "is again in these parts on one of her trips of mercy to God's poor," and to expect her arrival in the next day or so.[39] Station by station, Tubman conducted her last group of fugitives all the way to safety to the Canadian town of St. Catharines, where she took refuge among family members for the next five months.[40]

Harriet's responsibilities as an Underground Railroad conductor had now ended, but she was about to assume another, more militant role even as the United States would soon be divided by a bloody civil war.

NOTES

1. Harriet Tubman to Emma Telford, "Harriet: The Modern Moses of Heroism and Visions," (1911): 14. Cayuga County Historian's Office, Auburn, New York.

2. John Brown quoted in Lillie Chace Wyman, "Harriet Tubman," *New England Magazine* 6 (March 1896): 110–118.

3. Catherine Clinton, *Harriet Tubman: The Road to Freedom* (New York: Little, Brown, 2004), 124–125, 128.

4. Clinton, *Road to Freedom*, 128–129.

5. There are several excellent biographies of John Brown, including: W. E. Burghardt Du Bois, *John Brown* (Philadelphia: George W. Jacobs & Company, 1909); Stephen B. Oates, *To Purge This Land with Blood: A Biography of John Brown* (Amherst: University of Massachusetts, 1984); and David S. Reynolds, *John Brown, Abolitionist: The Man Who Killed Slavery, Sparked the Civil War, and Seeded Civil Rights* (New York: Knopf, 2006).

6. Edward J. Renehan, Jr., *The Secret Six: The True Tale of the Men Who Conspired with John Brown* (New York: Crown, 1995), 64–65.

7. David M. Potter, *The Impending Crisis, 1848–1861* (New York: Harper, 1976), 199–224.

8. Potter, *Impending Crisis*, 267–280.

9. Renehan, *The Secret Six*, 118–120.

10. Frederick Douglass, quoted in Stanley Campbell, *The Slave Catchers: Enforcement of the Fugitive Slave Law, 1850–1860* (Chapel Hill: University of North Carolina, 1968), 52–53.

11. Clinton, *Road to Freedom*, 127–128.

12. Milton C. Sernett, *Harriet Tubman: Myth, Memory, and History* (Durham, NC: Duke University Press, 2007), 78.

13. Letter, John Brown to John Brown, Jr., April 8, 1858, quoted in Frederick B. Sanborn, ed., *The Life and Letters of John Brown* (New York: Negro Universities, 1885), 452.

14. Clinton, *Road to Freedom*, 129–130.

15. Sernett, *Myth, Memory and History*, 79.

16. Larson, *Bound for the Promised Land*, 159; and Sernett, *Myth, Memory and History*, 79.

17. Larson, *Bound for the Promised Land*, 161–166.

18. Letter, Reverend Thomas W. Higginson to mother, Worcester, MA: May 1859, quoted in Bishop W. J. Walls, *Harriet Tubman* (Ithaca, New York: Cornell University Archives), 1.

19. Jean Humez, *Harriet Tubman: The Life and the Life Stories* (Madison: University of Wisconsin, 2003); *Harriet Tubman*, 34–39; and Clinton, *Road to Freedom*, 132.

20. Tubman, quoted in Humez, *Harriet Tubman*, 243.

21. Du Bois, *John Brown*, 308–337.

22. John Brown, quoted in *New York Tribune:* November 10, 1859.

23. Ednah Dow Cheyney, "Moses," *Freedmen's Record* (March 1865): 37.

24. Harriet Tubman, quoted in *The Commonwealth* (Boston): July 17, 1863.

25. Clinton, *Road to Freedom*, 116.

26. Larson, *Bound for the Promised Land*, 163.

27. Clinton, *Road to Freedom*, 117.

28. Clinton, *Road to Freedom*, 118. Margaret's daughter Alice Lucas is the source of this information. She wrote a series of letters disclosing information about Harriet's personal life to Earl Conrad, one of Tubman's early biographers. These letters can be found in the Tubman Collection of the Schomburg Center for Research on Black Culture, New York City.

29. See Clinton, *Road to Freedom*, 121; and Larson, *Bound for the Promised Land*, 198–199.

30. See "Petition for Harriet Tubman." Filed with Harriet Tubman War Service Testimonial Materials, Records of the House of Representatives. National Archives and Records Administration, Washington, D.C. (hereafter, "HR"). On November 10, 1894, Tubman appeared at the Cayuga County Courthouse to apply for a pension for her military service. She took an oath to tell the truth stating, "I never had any children, nor child by the soldier [Nelson Davis, her second husband], nor by John Tubman [her first husband]."

31. Clinton, *Road to Freedom*, 119.

32. Sarah H. Bradford, *Harriet Tubman: The Moses of Her People* (1886; reprint, Secaucus, NJ: Citadel Press, 1961), 119–128; and Scott Christianson, "The Battle for Charles Nalle," *American Legacy* 2 (Winter 1997), 31–35.

33. John Bell Robinson, *Pictures of Slavery and Anti-Slavery* (1863; reprint, Miami, FL: Mnemosyne Publishing, 1969), 323–324, 327, 331.

34. Clinton, *Road to Freedom*, 141–142.

35. Sarah H. Bradford, *Scenes in the Life of Harriet Tubman* (Auburn, NY: W. J. Moses, 1869), 36.

36. Clinton, *Road to Freedom*, 142–145.

37. Humez, *Harriet Tubman*, 42, 230–231; and Cheyney, "Moses," 35–36.

38. Franklin B. Sanborn, "Harriet Tubman," *Boston Commonwealth*: July 17, 1863; and Bradford, *Moses of Her People*, 53–57.

39. Letter, Thomas Garrett to William Still, Wilmington, DE: December 1, 1860, quoted in James A. McGowan, *Station Master on the Underground Railroad: The Life and Letters of Thomas Garrett* (Jefferson, NC: McFarland, 2005), 152–153.

40. Clinton, *Road to Freedom*, 145.

Chapter 6

GENERAL TUBMAN GOES
TO WAR, 1861–1865

The election of Abraham Lincoln, an antislavery Republican, to the presidency in 1860 provoked a chain of events that not only led to a bloody civil war, but also to Tubman's dream of emancipation. Lincoln won the presidency because the Democratic Party split into sectional factions over the issue of slavery. In the North, only Lincoln and Senator Stephen Douglas of Illinois held any popular appeal. In the South, the race was between U.S. Vice President John C. Breckinridge, a Democrat whose platform called for a national slave code protecting slavery throughout the United States, and Senator John Bell of Tennessee, the Constitutional Union Party candidate, who avoided all discussion of slavery in an attempt to raise the federal constitution and the Union above the schism that divided the Democratic Party. When all the ballots were counted, Lincoln captured just 40 percent of the popular vote. But his base of support in the populous Northern states allowed him to capture 180 electoral votes, enough to secure victory.[1]

Many Southerners believed Lincoln's victory spelled the end of their way of life because of his repeatedly stated intention to prevent the spread of slavery into the new Western territories. There was growing talk of secession until December 20, 1860, when South Carolina voted to withdraw from the Union. In a desperate attempt to prevent the secession of more Southern states, Senator William H. Seward, Harriet's Auburn neighbor and benefactor, introduced a compromise bill in Congress on December 24. Though Seward had been a champion of the antislavery cause, his bill provided for the return of fugitive slaves, the prosecution of Underground Railroad agents, and a congressional guarantee to protect slavery in the states where it already existed. There is no record of Harriet's response to the measure. But her abolitionist friends, fearing that Seward might compromise her for political reasons, urged her to flee to Canada. Harriet reluctantly agreed, though she refused to relocate her parents and other family members from Auburn where she had recently purchased a property from Seward.[2]

Over the next six weeks, several other Southern states joined the secessionist movement, including Mississippi, Florida, Alabama, Georgia, Louisiana, and Texas. Together, on February 7, 1861, they established the Confederate States of America, an independent, Southern slave republic, and elected Jefferson Davis of Mississippi as their first president.

Lincoln refused to acknowledge the new Confederacy or the secessionist movement when he assumed the presidency on March 4, 1861. He insisted that the Union was perpetual and that no state could withdraw from it. Instead, he considered the Southern states to be in rebellion and directed his attention at restoring the Union by reassuring Southerners that he would "not interfere with slavery in the states where it already existed."[3] A stalemate followed until April 12, when Confederate batteries shelled the federal garrison at Fort Sumter, South Carolina—rejecting Lincoln's effort to provision the fort—and forced the surrender of the Union commander. Shortly after, Lincoln called for 75,000 volunteers to put down the Southern rebellion. In response, the Upper South states of Virginia, Tennessee, North Carolina, and Arkansas joined the Confederacy. Battle lines had been drawn. What would become the bloodiest war in the history of the United States had begun.

Lincoln, from the outset, made clear that the aim of the war was to preserve the Union, not to end slavery. Curiously, Lincoln, who had been morally opposed to slavery throughout his political career, did nothing to abolish it when he became president. Instead, he believed

HARRIET TUBMAN.

General Tubman: Harriet Tubman in her Civil War uniform. She soon replaced the skirt with a loose-fitting "bloomer dress," as she called it. Woodcut by J. C. Darby, reproduced as the frontispiece to Sarah H. Bradford's 1869 biography, Scenes in the Life of Harriet Tubman. *(Used with Permission of Documenting the American South, The University of North Carolina at Chapel Hill Libraries.)*

that he did not have the constitutional authority to eliminate slavery because of the "right of each state to order and control its own domestic institutions."⁴ He followed this policy during the early years of the Civil War in order to retain the loyalty of the border states, the northernmost tier of slaveholding states: Maryland, Delaware, Kentucky, West Virginia, and Missouri. He also revoked orders by Union generals emancipating the slaves of Confederates in Missouri.⁵ It was a wise decision. Each of the border states controlled vital strategic assets. Missouri not only bordered the Mississippi River, but controlled the routes to the West. Kentucky controlled the Ohio River. The main railroad link to the West ran through Maryland and the hill region of western Virginia, which split from Virginia to become a free state in 1863. Delaware controlled access to Philadelphia, a key industrial center. Finally, Washington, D.C., already threatened by the Confederate Army to the south in Virginia, was bordered in all other directions by Maryland. Had the state seceded, the nation's capitol would have been surrounded by the enemy and the Confederacy would enjoy a distinct advantage in the war. Stationing Union troops along Maryland's crucial railroad lines, the president insured the state's loyalty by declaring martial law in Baltimore, arresting the suspected ringleaders of a pro-Confederate mob, and holding them without trial. These were the first violations of basic civil rights that occurred during the Civil War, but Lincoln justified them on the basis of national security.[6]

Lincoln continued to defend his stand on slavery during the 17 months of the war. When pressed to give his position in August 1862, Lincoln insisted that emancipation was a moot point. "If I could save the Union without freeing any slave, I would do it; and if I could save it by freeing some and leaving others alone, I would also do that," he wrote Horace Greeley, the influential abolitionist editor of the *New York Tribune*. "What I do about slavery and the colored race," he concluded, "I do because it helps to save the Union."[7]

Tubman was infuriated by Lincoln's refusal to make a firm commitment to abolitionism. She believed that Union victory in the Civil War was the key to emancipation. "God won't let master Lincoln beat the South till he does the right thing," she said, condemning the president's position.

> Master Lincoln, he's a great man, and I am a poor negro; but the negro can tell master Lincoln how to save the money and the young men. He can do it by setting the negro free. Suppose that was an awful big snake down there, on the floor. He bite you. Folks all scared because you die. You send for a doctor to cut the bite; but the snake, he rolled up there, and while the doctor doing it, he bite you *again*. The doctor dug out *that* bite; but while the doctor doing it, the snake, he spring up and bite you again; so he *keep* doing it, till you kill *him*. That's what master Lincoln ought to know.[8]

Harriet's position could be better understood by her own experience with slavery. She had suffered the evils of the peculiar institution. Her family had been separated because of it. She had been beaten, repeatedly, by the hand of the master. For her, slavery was *real* and *personal;* not an abstract concept to be debated in the halls of Congress, as so many white abolitionists viewed it. But Lincoln's reluctance to end slavery must also be understood in the context of his Constitutional responsibilities as president.

Lincoln had no choice but to proceed cautiously on the issue of slavery. While he had a strong moral revulsion against the institution, the idea of emancipating slaves by executive order went against his political instincts. He realized that he had been elected on an antislavery platform and he also understood that as president, he had sworn to uphold the federal Constitution, which placed strict limits on his ability to interfere with slavery.

What's more, Lincoln realized that a president who defied public opinion could lose his capacity to lead altogether and that most Northern whites viewed black people as inferior. Many also believed that emancipation would trigger a massive influx of former slaves into the North, where they would compete for white men's jobs. Race riots in New York, Philadelphia, and Buffalo dramatized these white attitudes. Under these circumstances, if Lincoln moved too quickly on emancipation, he risked offending the border states, and increased the Democrats' chances for reclaiming the White House in 1864. Yet if he didn't make a move, Lincoln would alienate abolitionists and lose the support of the Radical Republicans, which he simply could not afford to do.[9] Nevertheless, the president's reluctance angered Harriet, who began to consider the role she would play in the Civil War.

In October 1861, Harriet, who had been exiled to Canada, accepted an invitation to travel to Boston to meet with abolitionist Governor of Massachusetts John A. Andrew, a radical abolitionist. Andrew was eager to enlist the services of African Americans once the war began. He may have discussed the possibility of Harriet becoming a Union army spy and scout as early as this meeting. Her experience with the Underground Railroad would have made her an ideal candidate for such a dangerous and secretive mission. But there was no demand for her services in the early months of the war.[10]

Northern Virginia was the most crucial theater of battle, with the two enemy capitals of Washington and Richmond only 70 miles apart. Had the Army of the Potomac, under the command of General George C. McClellan, been more aggressive in attacking the Confederate armies, the North might have prevailed in the first year of the conflict. But McClellan, who was notoriously cautious, failed to engage the Confederates on the Virginia Peninsula, resulting in a stalemate. The Union Navy was more successful, seizing exposed coastal areas in South Carolina, Georgia, and Florida. While whites fled the area during the Union advance, the troops were welcomed by thousands of slaves, who had been freed unwittingly before any official policy from Washington. These *contrabands*, that is, slaves free by military action rather than civil law, were put to work building fortifications and working in Union camps. Union commanders had discovered a way to deprive the South of its basic labor force.[11] The capture of Port Royal in the South Carolina Sea Islands in November 1861 opened the door for Tubman's involvement in the war.

In May 1862, Tubman joined a group of Boston and Philadelphia abolitionists heading to Port Royal, one of the South Carolina's many Sea Islands. The Sea Islands were a fertile and productive plantation area that stretched along the coast from Charleston to Savannah, Georgia. This extensive region was home to 10,000 slaves, now contraband of war.[12] Lacking employment, property, and formal education, these contraband were in dire poverty. Tubman and other abolitionists assumed the responsibility of distributing clothes, food, and medicines to the newly freed slaves. Harriet became an indispensible part of the camps assisting fugitives, especially women, whom she taught to wash, sew, and bake for the Union soldiers as a means of earning wages.[13] She also served as a nurse, preparing remedies from indigenous plants and aiding soldiers suffering from contagious diseases like dysentery, smallpox, and measles.[14] Harriet described the situation in a letter she dictated and sent to Franklin B. Sanborn, editor of the Boston Commonwealth:

> Most of the contraband come from South Carolina to the Sea Islands and are very destitute, almost naked. I am trying to find places for those able to work, and provide for them as best I can, so as to lighten the burden of the Government as much as possible while at the same time they learn to respect themselves by earning their own living.[15]

Initially, Harriet received government rations for her work amounting to $200, which she immediately invested in building a laundry.[16] But when newly freed slaves accused her of receiving preferential treatment, she refused any further financial compensation and made money by baking pies and selling them to the soldiers. Whenever she made additional money, she sent the funds home for her parents.[17]

Major General David Hunter, commander of the Union Army's Department of the South, had other plans. Hunter believed that African Americans should and must serve in the Union Army. After freeing the contraband under martial law, he fully intended to organize them into a fighting unit. Similarly, in accordance with Governor Andrew's wishes, Hunter expected to utilize Harriet as a military spy. In fact, she had been under the impression that she would be employed in that capacity from the very beginning, but "they changed their program and wanted me to go down and distribute clothes to the contrabands who were coming in to the Union lines night and day."[18] It's possible that Harriet's humanitarian activities may have been a cover for her actual duties as a spy for the military. She may have been serving in a dual capacity, though there is no mention of her intelligence gathering until months after her arrival. By that time, Lincoln had revoked Hunter's order to free the contraband, fearing it would alienate the slaveholding border states that had remained loyal to the Union. His action outraged Harriet as well as the prominent black abolitionist, Frederick Douglass, who in a speech on July 4, 1862, denounced the president's motives:

> He [President Lincoln] has steadily refused to reclaim, as he had the constitutional and moral right to proclaim, complete emancipation to all the slaves of rebels who should make their way into the lines of our army. He has repeatedly interfered with and arrested the anti-slavery policy of some of his most earnest and reliable generals . . . It is from such action as this, that we must infer the policy of the Administration. To my mind that policy is simply and solely to reconstruct the union on the old and corrupting basis of compromise, by which slavery shall retain all the power that it ever had, with the full assurance of gaining more, according to its future necessaries.[19]

Tubman agreed with Douglass. She believed that until the slaves were freed, the Confederacy would continue to wage war against the Union and many more Northern lives would be lost. If, on the other hand,

Lincoln had the moral courage to free the slaves and use them on the battlefield, the Confederacy would be destroyed and countless lives spared.[20] It appeared, however, as if Harriet would have to wait until the political climate was more favorable to emancipation. But Lincoln was not deaf to their concerns.

As the casualty lists grew to appalling proportions, the president began to reconsider the meaning of the war in a way that went far beyond politics and public opinion. He began to question why the South was winning the war if, in fact, the will of God prevails. "God wills his contest, and wills that it should not end," he wrote in a September 1862 personal reflection known as his *Meditation on the Divine Will.* "By His mere quiet power, He could have either saved or destroyed the Union without human contest." Lincoln was now convinced that he was "an instrument in God's hands for accomplishing a great work" and he looked for some kind of sign to provide him with direction.[21] The president's sign arrived on September 17, 1862, with the Union victory at Antietam. Five days later, Lincoln, despite the divided opinion of his own cabinet, issued the Emancipation Proclamation, declaring that unless the rebellious states returned to the Union by January 1, 1863, he would declare their slaves "forever free."[22] When the Confederacy rejected his demand to free their slaves, Lincoln, on New Year's Day, 1863, issued the proclamation as he had promised, calling it an "act of justice warranted by the Constitution upon military necessity."[23]

Lincoln's purpose in issuing the proclamation was to meet the abolitionist demand for a war against slavery while not losing the support of conservatives. Accordingly, the Emancipation Proclamation had no immediate impact on slavery in the border states, affecting only those slaves who lived in the unconquered portions of the Confederacy. It was so equivocal that Lincoln's own Secretary of State, William Seward, remarked sarcastically, "We show our sympathy with slavery by emancipating slaves where we cannot reach them and holding them in bondage where we can set them free."

Still, the Emancipation Proclamation did represent a dramatic shift in Lincoln's view of the war. What had begun as a war to save the Union now also became a struggle that, if victorious, would free the slaves. It also liberated Lincoln from the sharp tension he once felt between those two objectives, and reflected his newfound realization that he could not save the Union "half free and half slave" as he had previously asserted. Though Harriet considered the proclamation an important step towards emancipation, she could not celebrate the long-overdue measure as long as slavery remained legal in her native Maryland, as well as in the other four border states. Instead, she became emboldened to defeat the Confederacy at all costs, sneaking into enemy territory and gathering intelligence for the Union Army. Under orders from Secretary of War Edwin M. Stanton, Harriet led a band of scouts through the marshlands around Port Royal, mapping the unfamiliar terrain and reconnoitering its inhabitants. Her efforts helped track Confederate movements and allowed the Union Army to pursue a successful guerilla campaign in the region.[24]

The Emancipation Proclamation also forced Lincoln to reconsider the role black troops might play in the outcome of the war. Strong opposition in the North, as well as a lingering prejudice that blacks were intellectually and socially inferior, limited most black involvement to driving supply wagons, burying the dead after battle, and building railroads for the war effort. Pressured by a series of Union defeats in 1862 and a drop in white enlistments, Congress repealed a 1792 ordinance barring "persons of color" from serving in the militia and passed a Confiscation Act that empowered the president to "use as many persons of African descent" as he needed "for the Suppression of the Rebellion." General Hunter was the first to act on the new legislation. With the help of Harriet Tubman, he recruited two regiments of contrabands and fugitives to serve under the command of Colonel James Montgomery.[25] Lincoln followed suit by allowing for the recruitment of a larger black army. Having freed by executive order those slaves in the South, the president could no longer deny the black man the opportunity to fight. When some Union generals complained about his change of heart, Lincoln was swift in his response. "You say you will not fight to free Negroes," he shot back. "Some of them seem to be willing to fight for you. When victory is won, there will be some black men who can remember that, with silent tongue and clenched teeth, and steady eye and well-poised bayonet, they helped mankind in to this great consummation. I fear, however, that there will also be some white ones, unable to forget that with malignant heart and deceitful speech, they strove to hinder it."[26]

Frederick Douglass, ca. 1848. Like Tubman, Douglass (1818–1895) had been born a slave on Maryland's Eastern Shore. (Courtesy of Chester County Historical Society, West Chester, PA)

On February 13, 1863, Senator Charles Sumner of Massachusetts presented a bill in Congress proposing the "enlistment of 300,000 colored troops." Although the bill was defeated, the state's governor, John Andrew, long a champion of a black army, requested and received authorization from Secretary of War Stanton to organize a colored regiment of volunteers to serve for three years. In Massachusetts, only 100 men volunteered during the first six weeks of recruitment. The state's black men were insulted by the fact that the regiment would be headed by only white officers and by the fact that black soldiers would receive lower pay than white soldiers. Disappointed by the number of volunteers, Andrew organized a committee of prominent citizens and black leaders to supervise the recruitment of black troops. Within two month's time, the committee had collected $5,000 and established recruiting posts from Boston to St. Louis. Soon the quota was raised, and 1,000 freed-men and former slaves from throughout the Union became part of the "54th Regiment Massachusetts Volunteer Colored Infantry" under the command of Colonel Robert Gould Shaw, the 25-year-old scion of a wealthy and socially prominent Boston abolitionist family. When they were first put into service, the black soldiers of the 54th were segregated in camp and given the worst jobs. Many white officers and soldiers treated them as inferiors. They were paid $10 a month, three dollars less than white soldiers. To protest, the 54th refused to accept pay, prefer-ring to serve for free until they were paid the same salary as white sol-diers. Their protest proved successful. In June 1864, the United States War Department equalized wages between black and white soldiers.[27] Meanwhile, Harriet had again shifted her responsibilities from military spy to soldier.

The federal army's Department of the South was responsible for hold-ing the Sea Islands, preventing foreign aid to the Confederacy by keep-ing the Union's naval blockade intact, and harassing the remaining Confederate troops throughout the Southeast. Their primary tactic was guerilla warfare, which required an intimate knowledge of the local terrain. Throughout the summer of 1863, the Union conducted many small-scale guerilla raids. Harriet was instrumental in the success of these operations. Having organized a band of African American spies and scouts, she and her troops prepared the groundwork for the raids, which were made by both black and white forces.[28] One of the largest and most effective campaigns occurred in the late spring of 1863, when Colonel Montgomery and his two contraband regiments of South Carolina Vol-unteers conducted an assault on a series of plantations along the Com-bahee River. It was during this operation that Tubman became the first woman to lead an armed assault during the Civil War.[29]

On the morning of June 2, Harriet guided three Union gunboats of some 300 black soldiers up the Combahee River. Tubman, who directed the advance intelligence gathering of the scouts, traveled in the lead boat with Montgomery, while one of her spies directed the craft around torpedoes that had been planted below the river's surface by the Con-federates. Once ashore, the soldiers met little resistance. They set fire to plantations and warehouses, destroying thousands of dollars of food and supplies. After the raid, steamboats appeared along the river and began sounding their whistles; a signal that the area was being liberated. Slaves flocked to the shoreline carrying whatever belongings they hold.[30] "I never saw such a sight," exclaimed Harriet. "Sometimes the women would come with twins hanging around their necks; it appears I never saw so many twins in my life; bags on their shoulders, baskets on their heads, and young ones tagging along behind, all loaded; pigs squealing, chickens screaming, young ones squealing." In an effort to assist one of the fleeing slaves, Harriet, carrying two pigs, raced to the river's edge and, in the process, "stepped on [her] long dress tearing it almost off." Afterward, she decided to change her "uniform." In the future she would go into battle dressed in a headscarf to cover her hair, a jacket, and "bloomers," or loose-fitting pants, to allow her to move more freely behind enemy lines.[31]

When Confederate troops finally raced to the scene, all they could do was watch as the steamboats full of newly liberated slaves sailed off toward Beaufort. The Combahee River raid earned Harriet even greater recognition. Not only did the raid deprive the Confederate Army of supplies they desperately needed to continue the war, but it also freed more than 750 slaves, many of whom joined the Union Army. When Harriet learned that the Northern newspapers had credited Colonel Montgomery with the success of the expedition, she had a letter written for her to Franklin Sanborn, a friend and the editor of a Boston antislavery newspaper, and complained about the omission of black involvement:

> You have, without doubt, seen a full account of the expedition. Don't you think we colored people are entitled to some credit for that exploit, under the lead of the brave Colonel Montgomery? We weakened the rebels somewhat on the Combahee River, by taking and bringing away seven hundred and fifty-six of their most valuable live-stock, known up in your region as "contrabands," and this, too, without the loss of a single life on our part.[32]

Sanborn apparently agreed and wrote a biographical sketch of Harriet and published it along with excerpts from her letter the following week.[33] Although she might not have been acknowledged by the newspapers, Tubman was respected by the black scouts she commanded as well as Union soldiers—both black and white—and officers who "never failed to tip their caps when meeting her."[34] Even Colonel Montgomery, who possessed an inflated sense of self-importance, credited her as "a most remarkable woman, and invaluable scout."[35]

Harriet's stature as a soldier was at its height in July when she was stationed at Camp Saxton where the 54th Massachusetts was encamped. Up to that time, the black regiment had been used primarily for manual labor, but when Colonel Shaw requested to lead a three-pronged attack to capture the heavily fortified islands that dotted Charleston's harbor, his men were pressed into service. The key to the attack was seizing control of Fort Wagner. If the garrison could be taken, the Union Army could launch a major assault further south on Fort Sumter, which controlled access to the harbor. From there, it would only be a matter of time before Charleston itself fell.[36] But Shaw realized that he had volunteered his men for a suicide mission. As the lead force in the attack, the 54th would suffer heavy casualties. Even if they made it inside the fort and survived the battle, those who were captured—including white officers—would be executed in accordance with an act of the Confederate Congress.[37]

The 54th's valiant assault on Fort Wagner took place on July 18, 1863. Harriet, who served as a cook and nurse at Camp Saxton, reportedly served Colonel Shaw and his men their last meal that morning.[38] Almost from the beginning the assault proved to be a bloody slaughter. "We saw the lightening, and that was the guns," said Harriet, comparing the battle to a raging storm. "And then we heard the thunder, and that was the big guns; and then we heard the rain falling, and that was the drops of blood falling; and when we came to get in the crops, it was dead men we reaped."[39] When the assault ended, the Union had lost 1,515 killed, wounded or missing. Of that number, 256 casualties were from the 54th Massachusetts, including commanding officer Colonel Robert Shaw, who was killed in action. That number represents almost 40 percent of the 650 men who served in the regiment. By comparison, the Confederates lost just 174 men.[40] From a military standpoint, the Union assault on Fort Wagner was a costly failure. But the effort proved to be a turning point for blacks, serving to lessen lingering skepticism among whites about the combat readiness of African Americans. The 54th's valiant example opened the ranks of the Union Army to nearly 200,000 black men (one out of every five African American males in the nation) who were organized into the U.S. Colored Troops between June 1863 and the end of the war in April 1865. One-fifth of those troops—37,000 men—died defending their own freedom and the Union.[41]

Harriet, who was sent to help bury the dead and nurse the survivors almost immediately after the failed assault, was exhausted.[42] She took a leave from her duties in the autumn of 1863 and returned home to Auburn to visit her parents, whom she hadn't seen for more than a year. When she returned to the battlefront, Harriet worked as a nurse in Virginia's military hospitals, which maintained separate facilities for black and white soldiers. She constantly complained about the unsanitary conditions experienced by wounded black soldiers:

> I'd go to the hospital early every morning. I'd get a big chunk of ice, and put it in a basin, and fill it with water; then I'd take a sponge and begin. First man I'd come to, I'd thrash away the flies, and they'd rise, they would, like bees around a hive. Then I'd begin to bathe the wounds, and by the time I'd bathed off three or four, the fire and heat would have melted the ice and made the water warm, and it would be as red as clear blood. Then I'd go and get more ice, and by the time I got to the next ones, the flies would be round the first ones black and thick as ever.[43]

When dysentery overwhelmed one of the black hospitals, Harriet concocted a tea remedy from local roots and herbs, and the epidemic soon dissipated.[44] Even after the war ended in April 1865, Harriet donated several more months of service to address the inequitable treatment of wounded black soldiers. Traveling to Washington, D.C., she met with the U.S. Surgeon General and told him of the deplorable conditions in the military hospitals that were maintained for black troops, noting that a wounded African American soldier was twice as likely to die as an injured white soldier. He promised to appoint Harriet the matron, or head nurse, of the black hospital at Fort Monroe, Virginia, and to send supplies to improve the unsanitary conditions there. But the appointment and supplies never materialized. She remained at Fort Monroe until July 1865, when she returned to Washington to make a final plea for help, and then went home to Auburn.[45]

Emancipation seemed to soften Harriet's view of President Lincoln. Her earlier disappointments in his reluctance to free the slaves and to give black soldiers the same pay as white ones yielded to deep personal grief after his assassination. "I didn't understand then [that] Master Lincoln was our friend," she recalled in later years. "It was Sojourner Truth [a runaway slave who became a noted abolitionist and preacher] who told me that he was our friend. She went to see him, and she thanked him for all he had done for our people. Yes, I'm sorry now that I didn't thank him, too."[46]

NOTES

1. David Herbert Donald, *Lincoln* (New York: Simon & Schuster, 1996 paperback), 256.

2. Jean Humez, *Harriet Tubman: The Life and the Life Stories* (Madison: University of Wisconsin, 2003), 45–46.

3. Abraham Lincoln, quoted in "First Inaugural Address," March 4, 1861, quoted in Henry Louis Gates, *Lincoln on Race & Slavery* (Princeton, NJ: Princeton University Press, 2009), 215–217.

4. Lincoln, "First Inaugural," 215.

5. James M. McPherson, *Abraham Lincoln and the Second American Revolution* (New York: Oxford, 1990), 127.

6. Mark E. Neeley, Jr., *The Fate of Liberty: Abraham Lincoln and Civil Liberties* (New York: Oxford University, 1991), 7–18.

7. Abraham Lincoln to Horace Greeley, Washington, D.C. (August 22, 1862) quoted in Gates, *Lincoln on Race & Slavery*, 243.

8. Tubman, quoted in Kate Clifford Larson, *Bound for the Promised Land: Harriet Tubman, Portrait of an American Hero* (New York: Ballantine Books, 2004), 206. Emphasis in the original.

9. John Hope Franklin, *The Emancipation Proclamation* (New York: Doubleday, 1963), 20.

10. Humez, *Harriet Tubman*, 49.

11. James Oliver Horton, and Lois E. Horton, *Slavery and the Making of America* (New York: Oxford University Press, 2005), 177–178.

12. Humez, *Harriet Tubman*, 50.

13. Larson, *Bound for the Promised Land*, 204.

14. Catherine Clinton, *Harriet Tubman: The Road to Freedom* (New York: Little, Brown, 2004), 157.

15. Dictated letter, Harriet Tubman to Franklin B. Sanborn, June 30, 1863, quoted in Kenneth W. Cameron, ed., *Correspondence of Franklin B. Sanborn the Transcendentalist* (Hartford, CT: Transcendental Books, 1982), 24.

16. William J. Walls, *Harriet Tubman* (Charlotte, NC: A.M.E. Zion Church, 1946), 9.

17. Clinton, *Road to Freedom*, 156–157.

18. Harriet Tubman, quoted in Emma P. Telford, "Harriet: The Modern Moses of Heroism and Visions." (ca. 1905) Typescript. Cayuga Museum and Case Research Lab Museum, Auburn, New York.

19. Frederick Douglass, quoted in James M. McPherson, *The Negro's Civil War: How American Negroes Felt and Acted during the War for the Union* (New York: Ballantine Books, 1991), 46.

20. Letter, Lydia Maria Child to John Greenleaf Whittier, January 21, 1862 quoted in Walls, *Harriet Tubman*, 8–9.

21. Abraham Lincoln, "Meditation on the Divine Will," ca. early September 1862 in *Abraham Lincoln: Speeches and Writings, 1859–1865*, ed. Don E. Fehrenbacher (New York: Library of America, 1989, 2 vols.), 2:359.

22. Abraham Lincoln, "Preliminary Emancipation Proclamation," September 22, 1862, *Speeches and Writings*, 2: 368–370.

23. Abraham Lincoln, "Final Emancipation Proclamation," January 1, 1863, *Speeches and Writings*, 2: 425.

24. Larson, *Bound for the Promised Land*, 210; Clinton, *Road to Freedom*, 164.

25. McPherson, *Negro's Civil War*, 167.

26. Abraham Lincoln quoted in Geoffrey C. Ward, *The Civil War* (New York: Alfred A. Knopf, 1990), 247.

27. Benjamin Quarles, *The Negro in the Civil War* (New York: Da Capo Press, 1989 paperback), 8–9. For a complete history of the 54th Massachusetts, see: Luis F. Emilio, *A Brave Black Regiment. History of the 54th Massachusetts Regiment* (1894; reprint, Salem, NH: Ayer Company, 1990).

28. Benjamin Quarles, *The Negro in the Civil War* (New York: Da Capo Press, 1989 paperback ed.), 226.

29. Larson, *Bound for Promised the Land*, 212.

30. Harriet Tubman, quoted in Dorothy Sterling, ed., *We Are Your Sisters: Black Women in the Nineteenth Century* (New York: Norton, 1984), 245–305.

31. Dictated letter of Harriet Tubman to Franklin B. Sanborn, June 30, 1863, quoted in Bradford, *Scenes in Life of Tubman*, 85–86.

32. Tubman to Sanborn, quoted in Bradford, *Scenes in Life of Tubman*, 86–87.

33. *Commonwealth* (Boston, MA): July 17, 1863.

34. William Wells Brown, *The Rising Son* (Boston: A. G. Brown, 1874), 536.

35. Letter, Colonel James Montgomery to General Quincy A. Gillmore, July 6, 1863, quoted in Quarles, *Negro in Civil War*, 227.

36. Peter M. Chaitin, *The American Civil War: The Coastal War from Chesapeake Bay to Rio Grande* (Alexandria, VA: Time-Life Books, 1984), 121–125.

37. See "Act of the Congress of the Confederate States of America," Section IV (May 1, 1863), in Luis F. Emilio, *A Brave Black Regiment: History of the 54th Massachusetts Regiment* (1894); reprinted Salem, NH: Ayer Company, 1990, 7.

38. Larson, *Bound for the Promised Land*, 220.

39. Tubman, quoted in Earl Conrad, *Harriet Tubman: Negro Soldier and Abolitionist* (New York: International Publishers, 1942), 40.

40. Emilio, *Brave Black Regiment*, 91.

41. Quarles, *Negro in the Civil War*, 20–21.

42. Humez, *Harriet Tubman*, 62.

43. Tubman, quoted in Humez, *Harriet Tubman*, 62.

44. Humez, *Harriet Tubman*, 63.

45. Charles P. Wood, "Narrative of Harriet Tubman War Service" (1868) HR.

46. Rosa Belle Holt, "A Heroine in Ebony," *Chautauquan* 23 (July 1896): 459–462.

Chapter 7

AUBURN, 1866–1886

In October 1865, Harriet boarded a late-night train in Philadelphia to return home to her family at Auburn, New York. She had recently resigned her position as a nurse at Fort Monroe, Virginia, realizing the impossibility of improving conditions at the military hospital without federal assistance.

Seated in a passenger car, she was approached by the conductor of the Camden & South Amboy train who told her to move to the smoking car. Harriet refused. Producing a soldier's pass for a half-fare train ticket, she politely explained that she had a right to the seat because of her government service. The conductor would not listen.

"Come hustle out of here!" he shouted, grabbing her by the arm. "We don't carry niggers for half-fare."

When she resisted, he began to curse at her.

"I'll thank you to call me 'black' or Negro, you copperhead scoundrel," she screamed back. "I'm just as proud of being a black woman as you are of being white!"

Other passengers watched intently as the ugly scene unfolded. No one came to her assistance, though some urged the conductor to throw her off the train, shouting: "Pitch the nigger out!"

Unable to jar Harriet from her seat, the conductor summoned two other passengers for help. While she clutched at the railing, the three men wrestled her loose and threw her into the baggage car. In the process, Harriet sustained a broken arm and several bruised ribs.[1]

It was a rude awakening to the realities of black citizenship in the United States and the introduction to a new chapter in Harriet's life. During the next half century she would emerge as a civil rights pioneer.

The Reconstruction Era, which lasted from 1865 to 1877, was a turbulent period in American history for blacks. Lacking consensus on how recently freed slaves, or "freedmen," would be integrated into the economic, social, and political life of the United States, the Republican-dominated Congress engaged in an ongoing battle with the Democratic president Andrew Johnson, who assumed executive leadership after the assassination of Abraham Lincoln in April 1865.

Johnson alienated antislavery Radical Republicans by proposing lenient measures to restore the Southern states to the Union and began implementing them during the summer of 1865.[2] By the end of the year all the seceded states had formed new governments and awaited congressional approval of them. But the Radicals refused to recognize Johnson's governments since Northern opinion had become hostile toward the South. Delegates elected to the Southern state conventions had been reluctant to abolish slavery and refused to grant black suffrage. Southern state legislatures showed their defiance by electing former Confederate leaders to represent them in Congress. They also enacted a series of Black Codes, which prohibited freedmen from owning or leasing farms, and from taking any jobs other than plantation workers or domestic servants. The Black Codes also sanctioned arresting and fining unemployed blacks, and hiring them out to private employers to pay the fines.[3] Congress responded to these actions by establishing measures designed to protect the civil rights of the freedmen and delaying the readmission of the former Confederate states until these safeguards were in place. The Radicals began by expanding the powers of the Freedmen's Bureau—a federal agency created during the war to assist former slaves in adapting to free society—to include schools, medical care for the sick, and access to the judicial system.[4] When Johnson vetoed the measure, Congress overrode him, setting up an antagonistic pattern that would continue until Johnson was impeached in the spring of 1868.[5]

In April 1866, Congress passed the first Civil Rights Act, which declared blacks to be United States citizens and granted the federal government the authority to intervene in state affairs to protect their rights as citizens. Again, Johnson vetoed both bills and Congress overrode him. The same month, Congress approved the Fourteenth Amendment granting every U.S. citizen all the "privileges and immunities" guaranteed by the Constitution as well as equal protection under the law by both the state and national governments. Implicit in the amendment was the right to vote. Readmission would be granted to any Southern state that ratified the Fourteenth Amendment. Only Tennessee agreed, temporarily leaving Congress without the approval of three-fourths of the states needed for ratification of the amendment.[6]

The 1866 congressional elections marked a turning point in the Reconstruction process. Voters returned an overwhelming majority of Republicans to Congress, most of them Radicals.[7] Armed with a mandate, the Republicans, in early 1867, passed a coherent plan of their own over the objections of Johnson. Under the plan, the South was divided into five military districts, each with a military commander. Qualified voters—adult black males and white males who had not participated in the rebellion—were registered to elect delegates to state conventions that would draft new constitutions including provisions for black suffrage. After the new constitutions were ratified, voters could elect state governments. Congress had to approve each of the new constitutions. Once enough states ratified the Fourteenth Amendment to make it part of the Constitution, then the former Confederate states would be restored to the Union.[8]

Meanwhile, freedmen struggled to find work, land, and education in the postwar South. Whites became increasingly antagonistic toward the former slaves, trying to force them into a subordinate status as sharecroppers who worked for white landlords for meager pay. Secret societies, like the Ku Klux Klan, were established to intimidate freedmen. Blacks who refused to abide by traditional codes of racial etiquette were terrorized. Those who showed signs of political activism were lynched. Essentially, the KKK served as the paramilitary arm of the Southern Democratic Party in its effort to restore white supremacy to the South. Their terrorist actions, along with the existence of the Black Codes, instigated bloody race riots in New Orleans and several other Southern cities.[9]

Violence against freedmen was not limited to the Deep South either. Border states, like Maryland, also witnessed racial conflict as whites struggled with the directives imposed by Radical Republican Reconstruction.[10] John Tubman, Harriet's estranged husband, became a victim of the violence. On September 30, 1867, Tubman got into an argument with Robert Vincent, a white neighbor, over the "removal of some ashes from a tenant-house on Vincent's farm." Vincent went after Tubman with an ax, threatening to kill him. Although Tubman escaped, the two resumed their quarrel that evening when they met each other on a road outside of Cambridge. Vincent drew a pistol and fired a single shot into Tubman's forehead, killing him instantly.[11] Vincent was arrested and tried for murder. At the trial, he claimed that Tubman attacked him and that he acted in self-defense. The state's case against Vincent, however, rested on the testimony of Tubman's 13-year-old son, who apparently witnessed the killing. He proved to be unconvincing for the all-white jury and Vincent was acquitted. Afterward, the liberal newspaper, *The Baltimore American*, insisted that the acquittal was a fait accompli since the jury was "composed exclusively of Democrats" and used the incident to promote the necessity of black suffrage:

> That Vincent murdered the deceased we presume no one doubts; but as no one but a colored boy saw him commit the deed, it was universally conceded that he would be acquitted, the moment it was ascertained that the jury was composed exclusively of Democrats. The Republicans have taught the Democrats as much since 1860. They trashed them into at least a seeming respect for the Union. They educated them up to a tolerance of public schools. They forced them to recognize Negro testimony in their courts. But they haven't got them to the point of convicting a fellow Democrat for killing a Negro. But even that will follow when the Negro is armed with the ballot.[12]

To be sure, black suffrage was a contentious issue across the nation, not just in the South. White Northerners may have accepted emancipation, but they retained their traditional racial prejudices. Segregation continued in most Northern theaters, restaurants, streetcars, and schools. Black voting was also rejected by Northern voters in Connecticut, Kansas, Minnesota, Ohio, and Wisconsin. Northern whites resented the Radicals' imposition of black suffrage and were convinced that, given the chance, Southern whites would quickly strip blacks of the right to vote. Emboldened by their victory in the 1868 congressional elections, however, the Republicans passed the Fifteenth Amendment to the Constitution, which explicitly forbid the states from denying the vote to any citizen on account of "race, color, or previous condition of servitude." The amendment brought Reconstruction directly into the North by overturning the state laws that discriminated against black voters. In addition, Congress required the ratification of the Fifteenth Amendment as a condition for readmission to the Union for the last three Confederate states—Virginia, Mississippi, and Texas—which had not yet complied with the Reconstruction Acts. On March 30, 1870, after those three states were restored to the Union, the Fifteenth Amendment became part of the federal constitution and racial criteria for voting were banned throughout the United States.[13]

While Reconstruction added three important amendments to the Constitution that transformed civil rights and electoral laws throughout the nations, it still left Southern blacks unprotected in a hostile society. After securing the Fifteenth Amendment, Republications washed their hands of Reconstruction, and white Southern Democrats, called "Redeemers," took control of the state governments, excluding blacks from any real political power.[14]

As these events played out across the national stage, Harriet Tubman was establishing a home for herself at Auburn in Cayuga County. Located in central upstate New York, Auburn was part of an area known as the Burned Over District, where the religious revivals of the Second Great Awakening spread like wildfire among Protestants in the 1820s and 1830s. The evangelical impulses of the revival inspired a humanitarian spirit that expressed itself most clearly in the 1850s in the abolitionist activities of such residents as Frederick Douglass, Gerrit Smith, Beriah Green, Jermain Loguen, and Samuel May. These abolitionists, and many lesser-known reformers, established an interracial network that rescued fugitives from slave hunters and maintained safe houses on the Underground Railroad.[15] Tubman, who often relied on these agents during her rescue missions, was now their neighbor. Financially destitute, she would also come to rely on them for charity.

Since escaping slavery in 1849, Harriet's humanitarianism kept her in a perpetual state of poverty. Despite years of service for the cause of emancipation, she never received a regular salary. In addition, her unofficial status during the Civil War created considerable difficulty in documenting her service, and the U.S. government was slow in recognizing its debt to her.[16] As a result, Harriet would struggle to support herself and her family. The winter of 1865 was an especially difficult one for her. In addition to her elderly parents, several relatives lived in her small house on South Street. The injuries she sustained on the Camden-South Amboy train prevented her from working for months. Harriet had to rely on the charity of her neighbors to feed her family that winter and even resorted to burning wood from the fences that surrounded her property for firewood.

Once, she walked to market carrying an empty basket. It was near the end of the business day and the vendors, eager to be rid of their produce, were offering it at a reduced price.

"Old woman," cried a butcher, "don't you want a nice piece of meat?"

"Here's a nice piece for just ten cents," cried another.

"Take this soup bone, you can have it for five cents," yelled another butcher.

But Harriet was broke. The butcher, noting her embarrassment, offered her the soup-bone on credit.

"Look here, old woman," said the first butcher, "you look like an honest woman; take this meat and pay me when you get some money."

Soon, Harriet's basket was full of meat and the vendors were declining payment altogether.

On her way home, Harriet passed a vegetable stand and exchanged some of the meat for potatoes, cabbage, and onions. That night, she prepared a magnificent stew for her family.[17]

On other occasions, a visit to a neighbor's house provided the sustenance she required. Townspeople readily invited Harriet into their homes, viewing her as a novelty because of her exceptionally dark complexion, remarkable background, and colorful storytelling. "She was a magnificent looking woman," recalled Helen Tatlock, a resident of Auburn. "She was a true African, very black with a broad nose and had a soft, colored voice. I used to often sit and listen to her stories when I could get her to tell them. We always gave her something to eat. She preferred butter in her tea to anything else. That was a luxury. She was a compelling character. She usually wore a full black skirt and an old black hat. She was not particular about her dress. She was, however, clean, but terribly poor."[18]

Once the winter passed and she was healed, Harriet supported her family by growing and selling vegetables, raising chickens, making baskets, caring for children, hiring herself out as a domestic to clean the homes, and taking in boarders.[19] One of the boarders was a young Civil War veteran named Nelson Davis. Davis, once a slave in Elizabeth City, North Carolina, escaped bondage around 1860 and settled in Oneida County, New York. He enlisted in the Eighth United States Colored Troops in 1863 and saw action at the Battle of Olustee, Florida. Honorably discharged on November 10, 1865, Davis relocated to Auburn where he found work as a brickmaker.[20] Not long after Davis

Tubman with seven dependents at Auburn, NY, ca. 1887: Left to right, Harriet Tubman, adopted daughter Gertie Davis, husband Nelson Davis, Lee Chaney, "Pop" Alexander, Walter Green, "Blind" Aunty Sarah Parker, and grandniece Dora Stewart. (Courtesy of the Friends Historical Library of Swarthmore College)

The Harriet Tubman Home in Auburn, NY, ca. 1908. (Courtesy of Cayuga Community College)

began boarding at Harriet's home, she learned of John Tubman's death. Though Davis was just 25 years old—and 22 years younger than Harriet—they soon fell in love. On March 18, 1869, the couple was married at the Central Presbyterian Church. Davis established a brick-making business on their property, but it proved to be unsuccessful. His frequent illnesses left him unable to work, and the water from the brickworks flooded Harriet's garden, making it difficult for her to grow crops for her family's subsistence.[21]

Again, Tubman turned to friends for charity. They responded by raising funds for her and her family. One white admirer, Sarah H. Bradford, the daughter of a New York State lawyer, legislator and judge, who operated a school for girls in Geneva, wrote an authorized biography titled *Scenes in the Life of Harriet Tubman*. It originated as a fundraising project and was encouraged by Harriet's friends, who realized that the book could be profitably sold at antislavery conventions (After the Thirteenth Amendment was passed civil rights advocates continued to hold fairs and conventions to raise money for freedmen). Published in 1869, the 132-page volume turned a profit of $1,200, which Tubman devoted to household finances and paying off the mortgage on the property she purchased from Senator William Seward.[22] Bradford was not a biographer; she was a writer of children's books. In the 1850s, she published several collections of stories for children that were best known for the moral lessons they inculcated in young minds.[23] Lacking the skill of a trained historian, Bradford relied on a series of interviews she did with Tubman in 1868 and failed to do the research necessary to corroborate Harriet's recollections. As a result, *Scenes* was hastily composed and reads more like a scrapbook of the highlights of Harriet's life and testimonial letters from abolitionist friends, than a carefully researched biography. It also exaggerates many events and portrays Tubman as a suffering saint:

> Worn down by her sufferings and fatigue, her health permanently affected by the cruelties to which she has been subjected, she is still laboring to the utmost limit of her strength for the support of her aged parents, and still also for her afflicted people . . . never obtruding herself, never asking for charity, except for "her people." . . . This woman of whom we have been reading is poor, and partially disabled from her injuries, yet she supports cheerfully and uncomplainingly herself and her own parents, and always has several poor children in her house, who are dependent entirely upon her exertions.[24]

Criticized by recent Tubman biographers for its artistic license, the book contains many factual inaccuracies as well as an extremely subjective perspective. Bradford revised and reissued the biography in 1886 at Harriet's request to again help alleviate dire financial circumstances. The revised volume was titled *Harriet, the Moses of Her People* and, like Bradford's first effort, it falls short of capturing the real Harriet Tubman. *Moses of Her People* is replete with racist language and stereotypes, as reflected in its opening pages:

> On a hot summer's day, perhaps sixty years ago, a group of merry little darkies were rolling and tumbling in the sand in front of the large house of a Southern planter. Their shining skins gleamed

in the sun, as they rolled over each other in their play, and their
voices, as they chattered together, or shouted in glee, reached
even to the cabins of the negro quarter, where the old people
groaned in spirit, as they thought of the future of those unconscious young revelers; and their cry went up, "O Lord, how long!"
Apart from the rest of the children, on the top rail of a fence,
holding tight onto the tall gate post, sat a little girl of perhaps
thirteen years of age; darker than any of the others, and with a
more decided *wooliness* in the hair; a pure unmitigated African.
She was not so entirely in a state of nature as the rollers in the
dust beneath her; but her only garment was a short woolen skirt,
which was tied around her waist, and reached about to her knees.
She seemed a dazed and stupid child, and as her head hung upon
her breast, she looked up with dull blood-shot eyes towards her
young brothers and sisters, without seeming to see them. Bye and
bye the eyes closed, and still clinging to the post, she slept.

The other children looked up and said to each other, "Look at
Hatt, she's done gone off agin." Tired of their present play ground
they trooped off in another direction, but the girl slept on heavily, never losing her hold on the post, or her seat on her perch.
Behold here, in the stupid little negro girl, the future deliverer of
hundreds of her people; the spy, and scout of the Union armies;
the devoted hospital nurse; the protector of hunted fugitives; the
eloquent speaker in public meetings; the cunning eluder of pur-
suing man hunters; the heaven-guided pioneer through dangers
seen and unseen; in short, as she has well been called, "The Moses
of her People."[25]

Bradford was, no doubt, painting a contrast between Harriet's crude,
humble beginnings and the tremendous success she would achieve later
in life. While the passage was intended to reflect the author's admiration for her subject, it played to the stereotypical characterizations of
blacks that were popular in post-Reconstruction America. Such literary license makes it difficult to determine what Harriet Tubman actually told Bradford about her life.

What's worse, Bradford, in her effort to accommodate a racist reading audience, gives Harriet the dialect of an ignorant field slave. The

following passage, for example, quotes Tubman on her first experience of crossing the Mason-Dixon Line into the free state of Pennsylvania in 1849: "I looked at my hands," she said, "to see if I was de same pusson now I was free. Dere was such a glory ober eberything, de sun came like gold trou de trees, and ober de fields, and I felt like I was in Heaben."[26] To be sure, Bradford considered herself to be one of Harriet's most loyal friends and defenders. But she was also a product of a Northern society that held white supremacist views. While her effort to elevate Harriet in the esteem of white readers was genuine, the vocabulary Bradford chose reflected those views:

I have often heard it said by Southern people that "niggers had no feeling; they did not care when their children were taken from them." I have seen enough of them to know that their love for their offspring is quite equal to that of the "superior race," and it is enough to hear the tale of Harriet's endurance and self-sacrifice to rescue her brothers and sisters, to convince one that a heart, truer and more loving than that of many a white woman, dwelt in her bosom. I am quite willing to acknowledge that she was almost an anomaly among her people, but I have known many of her family, and so far as I can judge they all seem to be peculiarly intelligent, upright and religious people, and to have a strong feeling of family affection. There may be many among the colored race like them; certainly all should not be judged by the idle, miserable darkies who have swarmed about Washington and other cities since the War.[27]

These racial stereotypes and factual inaccuracies were replicated in many subsequent biographies of Harriet Tubman because the writers accepted Bradford's two books uncritically. It's a shame that Harriet did not write her own life story. Tubman once confided to a friend that she had "hoped to learn to read and write after the [Civil] war" so that she could "write about her own life," but she never achieved that goal. In addition, the sporadic sleeping spells she experienced prevented her from "applying closely to a book."[28] There were other contemporaries, however, who would have been more credible authors than Bradford. Either William Still or Frederick Douglass would have been excellent candidates to write Tubman's biography. Both men shared a deep concern for helping fugitive slaves as well as recording and documenting the history of black people. More important, both Still and Douglass were African American and less influenced by the post-Reconstruction national dialogue on race, which blamed the victim, as the phrase goes, for slavery. Instead, later biographers were left to struggle with Bradford's two accounts in their attempts to extract the realities of Tubman's life from the mythology her first biographer created.[29]

Despite the charity of friends and neighbors, Harriet continued to struggle financially throughout the 1870s and 1880s. As a result, she fell prey to a swindle involving gold that was said to have been lost after the Civil War. In 1873, two black men, one named Stevenson and the other John Thomas, approached Harriet's brother, John Henry Stewart, claiming to have in their possession a cache of gold coins smuggled out of South Carolina.[30] Stating that the treasure was worth $5,000, they

Sarah H. Bradford (1818–1912) wrote Scenes in the Life of Harriet Tubman, *the first book-length treatment of Tubman's life, in 1868. (Courtesy of Geneva Historical Society)*

said that they could not be seen with the money and would trade it for $2,000 in cash. It appeared to be a legitimate offer.

Millions of dollars in gold was said to have been buried by individual planters and the Confederate government during the Civil War in order to prevent the Union from seizing it. Harriet was also aware that free black men were assigned the duty of digging graves for Union soldiers during the war and that these two men might have discovered the treasure in that capacity. In addition, they earned her trust by insisting that they knew one of her relatives.[31] Convinced by their story, Harriet borrowed $2,000 from a wealthy friend, Anthony Shimer, and arranged for the transfer late one night. Once the men had lured her into the woods, they made her unconscious with chloroform, bound and gagged her, and stole the $2,000. When she was found by her family, she was dazed and injured, and the money was gone.[32]

Harriet and her brother were briefly suspected of conspiring with the thieves to steal Shimer's money. But they assured the authorities that "no other arrangement was made than that of giving Shimer the benefit of the difference between greenbacks and gold." In addition, Shimer claimed that Harriet offered her house as collateral for the loan of the money. Together with Harriet's reputation for strict integrity among her white friends, these assurances convinced the authorities that she was telling the truth.[33] The incident aroused public sympathy for Harriet. Grateful for her past service and saddened by her economic woes, Representative Gerry W. Hazleton of Wisconsin introduced a bill of the floor of Congress providing that Tubman be paid "the sum of $2,000 for services rendered by her to the Union Army as scout, nurse, and spy." Unfortunately, the measure was defeated.[34] To generate income, Harriet continued to operate a farm growing vegetables, potatoes, and apples, and she sold eggs and chickens. She also continued to open her home to boarders and poor blacks seeking refuge.

By the mid-1870s, Harriet was the head of a crowded household. In addition to her mother, she took in four boarders including a 75-year-old blind widow. But the most valued addition arrived in 1874 when Harriet and Nelson adopted a baby girl named Gertie. Given the surname "Davis," the infant quickly fulfilled Harriet's long desire to be a mother to her own daughter.[35] There are indications that Harriet was not only a caring, but a fun-loving and playful parent. Known for her colorful storytelling, she would often add spontaneous, dramatic gestures. Harriet's grandniece, Alice Brickler, recalls one occasion when her elderly aunt got down on the ground and imitated a snake:

> [Aunt Harriet] and mother were talking as they say in the yard. Tiring of their conversation, I wandered off in the tall grasses to pick the wild flowers. Suddenly I became aware of something moving toward me through the grass. So smoothly did it glide and with so little noise, I was frightened! Then reason conquered fear and I knew it was Aunt Harriet, flat on her stomach and with only the use of her arms and serpentine movements of her body, gliding smoothly along. Mother helped her back to her chair and they laughed. Aunt Harriet then told me that that was the way she had gone by many a sentinel during the [Civil] war.[36]

Unfortunately, Harriet experienced more setbacks during the 1880s, beginning with the death of her mother, Rit, in October 1880. Rit, who was nearly a century old, was born a slave, but thanks to Harriet had spent the last third of her life as a free woman, surrounded by family and friends. Tubman's extended family had grown considerably since first settling in Auburn. Her niece, Margaret Stewart, married Henry Lucas, a local caterer, and the couple began their own family. Two of her nephews—William Henry Stewart, Jr., and John Henry Stewart— also married and started families. All three Stewart siblings settled into a close-knit black neighborhood, joining the extended families of Tubman's other friends, many of whom were fugitives from the Eastern Shore of Maryland.[37] Family and friends offered Harriet the emotional support she'd needed as she confronted the challenges of old age.

Sometime after 1882, Harriet's wood-framed farmhouse was destroyed by fire and many of her most cherished possessions went with it, including a collection of letters from noted abolitionists and Union officers.[38] Family members enlisted the help of local bricklayers to build a new brick home on the same site. Nelson managed to complete some of the work himself, though his health was rapidly declining from tuberculosis.[39]

Surrounded by family and friends, Harriet soldiered on. The Bradford biographies had introduced her to a younger generation of reformers and she found herself in demand for speaking engagements. She would spend the last part of her life as a voice for women's rights and an advocate for the elderly and poor.

NOTES

1. Letter, Martha Coffin Wright to Marianne Pelham Mott, November 7, 1865. Garrison Family Papers, Sophia Smith Collection, Smith College, Northampton, Massachusetts.

2. Eric Foner, *Reconstruction: America's Unfinished Revolution, 1863–1877* (New York: Harper & Row, 1988), 176–184.

3. Foner, *Reconstruction*, 199–201.

4. Kenneth M. Stampp, *The Era of Reconstruction, 1865–1877* (New York: Vintage, 1965; paperback), 132.

5. Stampp, *Era of Reconstruction*, 150–154.

6. Foner, *Reconstruction*, 118–119, 253–261.

7. Foner, *Reconstruction*, 260–271.

8. Stampp, *Era of Reconstruction*, 144–146.

9. Stampp, *Era of Reconstruction*, 199–201.

10. Foner, *Reconstruction*, 120.

11. "A Colored Man Murdered," *Baltimore American:* October 7, 1867. Harriet learned of the death of John Tubman in October 1867. She hadn't communicated with him since 1852 when she returned to the Eastern Shore and he spurned her offer to relocate in the North.

12. "Acquittal of Murderer," *Baltimore American:* December 23, 1867.

13. Foner, *Reconstruction*, 446–447.

14. Foner, *Reconstruction*, 587–600.

15. Milton C. Sernett, *North Star Country: Upstate New York and the Crusade for African American Freedom* (Syracuse, NY: Syracuse University, 2002).

16. Catherine Clinton, *Harriet Tubman: The Road to Freedom*. New York: Little, Brown, 2004, 193–195; and Kate Clifford Larson, *Bound for the Promised Land: Harriet Tubman, Portrait of an American Hero*

(New York: Ballantine Books, 2004), 276–277. Tubman did not receive a pension for her service in the Civil War until 1899 (see Larson, *Bound for the Promised Land*, 278–279).

17. Bradford, *Moses of Her People*, 143–145.

18. Letter, Helen Tatlock to Earl Conrade, September 9, 1939. Earl Conrad / Harriet Tubman Collection, Schomburg Center for Research in Black Culture, New York Public Library.

19. Jean Humez, *Harriet Tubman: The Life and the Life Stories* (Madison: University of Wisconsin, 2003), 78.

20. Larson, *Bound for the Promised Land*, 239.

21. Clinton, *Road to Freedom*, 198.

22. Clinton, *Road to Freedom*, 196.

23. Humez, *Harriet Tubman*, 146.

24. Sarah H. Bradford, *Scenes in the Life of Harriet Tubman* (Auburn, NY: W. J. Moses, 1869), 2, 103–104.

25. Sarah H. Bradford, *Harriet Tubman: The Moses of Her People* (1886; reprint, Secaucus, NJ: Citadel Press, 1961), 13–14.

26. Bradford, *Moses of Her People*, 30.

27. Bradford, *Moses of Her People*, 68–69.

28. Tubman, quoted by Ednah Dow Cheney, "Moses," *Freedmen's Record* 1 (March 1865): 38.

29. See James A. McGowan, "Harriet Tubman: According to Sarah Bradford," *Harriet Tubman Journal* (1994): 16; and Milton C. Sernett, *Harriet Tubman: Myth, Memory, and History* (Durham, NC: Duke University Press, 2007), 105–130.

30. Clinton, *Road to Freedom*, 201; and Larson, *Bound for the Promised Land*, 255–256.

31. Larson, *Bound for the Promised Land*, 256; and Clinton, *Road to Freedom*, 201.

32. Clinton, *Road to Freedom*, 201; and Larson, *Bound for the Promised Land*, 257–259.

33. Humez, *Harriet Tubman*, 89.

34. U.S. Representative Gerry W. Hazleton, quoted in Clinton, *Road to Freedom*, 202.

35. Larson, *Bound for the Promised Land*, 260. Very little is known of Gertie Davis except that she married a man named Watson in 1900.

36. Letter, Alice H. Brickler to Earl Conrad, July 28, 1939. Earl Conrad / Harriet Tubman Collection.

37. Larson, *Bound for Promised the Land*, 261.

38. "Harriet Tubman," *Boston Herald*: October 31, 1886.

39. Clinton, *Road to Freedom*, 203.

Chapter 8

LAST YEARS, 1887–1913

During the last part of her life, Harriet Tubman came to rely on the African American church for spiritual guidance as well as for social reform needs. At a time when independent black churches played a key role in mediating the racial divide in the industrial North, Harriet enlisted the support of the African Methodist Episcopal Church in meeting the needs of an underserved black population.

When Harriet first relocated her parents to Auburn, New York, in 1859, she attended the town's Central Presbyterian Church. Known for its antislavery activities, the church claimed among its congregants many of her white political allies.[1] In fact, she and Nelson Davis were married there in 1869. But the following year Nelson was elected a trustee of the A.M.E. Zion Church and she decided to join the congregation there.[2] By the end of the 1870s, Harriet was one of the most devoted congregants of the church. Apparently, she also possessed an exemplary religious zeal.

One congregant recalled Harriet's enthusiastic response to a scriptural reading at a service in the late 1870s. "In a shrill voice, she commenced to give testimony to God's goodness and long suffering," he said. "Soon she was shouting, and so were others also. She possessed such endurance, vitality, and magnetism that I inquired and was informed it was Harriet

Tubman—the 'Underground Railroad Moses.'" After the service, he introduced himself to her and she asked if he was saved. When he said that he was, Harriet cried out: "Glory to God!"[3]

Tubman recruited the congregation to help build a shelter and nursing care home for elderly African Americans that would be called John Brown Hall. Since most similar institutions were founded by whites, few accepted destitute elderly blacks. Many of these were former slaves who had lost contact with their family during slavery, and were left to face old age alone. Harriet's own experience in caring for the sick, disabled, and elderly acquainted her with the special hardships and needs of these people. She transformed her own home on South Street into an informal self-help community for them, employing the able-bodied members of the household to care for those who were invalid. By the late 1880s, her home was described as a "hospital for the infirm and sick" where she "cares for three or four invalids at a time."[4]

In June 1886, Tubman attempted to purchase land for a separate nursing home. She bid on an adjacent 25-acre farm property that was being auctioned off. It was a reckless effort since she did not have the money to cover her bid, and she was antagonized by the white bidders, but she prevailed. Harriet recounted the story to Sarah Bradford, who was preparing yet another revision of her biography in 1901:

> They was all white folks. There I was like a blackberry in a pail of milk, but I was hid down in a corner, and no one knowed who was bidding. The man began pretty low, and I kept going up by fifties. He got up to twelve hundred, thirteen hundred, fourteen hundred, and still that voice in the corner kept going up by fifties. At last it got up to fourteen hundred and fifty, and then others stopped bidding, and the man said, "All done! Who is the buyer?" "Harriet Tubman," I shouted. "What! That old nigger?" they said. "Old woman, how are you ever going to pay for that lot of land?" "I'm going home to tell the Lord Jesus all about it," I said.[5]

Tubman turned to the church for help. She asked the bishop of the A.M.E. Zion church conference at Syracuse to help her secure a $350 down payment as well as a bank mortgage loan for $1,000. In addition, Harriet asked Bradford to collaborate on a new edition of her biography and she embarked on a series of public appearances in order to raise funds for the project.[6] Many of her appearances came before women's suffrage groups, which viewed Tubman as the embodiment of female independence. Harriet immediately became one of the most popular speakers in a movement that had been closely affiliated with abolitionism since the 1840s.

Many of the women who became involved in the antislavery movement in the 1820s and 1830s came to resent the social and legal restrictions that limited their participation. Such middle–class reformers as Susan B. Anthony, Catharine Beecher, Dorothea Dix, Sarah and Angelina Grimke, Lucretia Mott, Elizabeth Cady Stanton, and Harriet Beecher Stowe chafed at claims by male abolitionists that their activism was inappropriate to their gender. They were educated women who worked as authors, editors, and orators. Their involvement in reform organizations gave them experience in running meetings, keeping accounts, maintaining records, and honing their skills as public speakers. Married women could not hold property or make contracts in their own names, so most women would not be able to accumulate the money to fund their reform organizations. But *these* particular women were the wives and daughters of wealthy and influential men who shared their views. They could use their social position to obtain donations and even special charters that allowed them to function legally as males; and they did. In doing so, they pressed the boundaries of "acceptable" female behavior by participating actively in the public discourse on slavery.[7] At the same time, they realized that there were limits to the authority that their social position could confer.

Women engaged in controversial reforms like abolitionism were often heckled and hounded by mobs. They were even subjected to criticism from within their own ranks. Some male abolitionists accused them of being an embarrassment to the movement. Disappointed by the refusal of these male abolitionists to abandon the traditional view and accept women as their peers in moral reform, Anthony, Beecher, Dix, Mott, Stanton, Stowe, and the Grimke sisters promoted women's rights, giving rise to a new consciousness of a female's precarious status in antebellum society. The turning point came in 1840 when American female delegates arrived at the world antislavery convention in London, only to be turned away by the men who controlled the proceedings. Angered by the rejection, Mott, Stanton, and others began to identify pointed parallels between the plights of women and the plight of slaves.[8] Their efforts came to fruition on July 19–20, 1848, at the Wesleyan Chapel in Seneca Falls, New York, where a convention was held to discuss the question of women's rights.

Three hundred people—including 40 men—attended the Seneca Falls Convention. By the end of the second day, the gathering had debated, voted on, and passed a "Declaration of Sentiments" modeled on the Declaration of Independence:

> We hold these truths to be self-evident: that all men and women are created equal. . . . The history of mankind is a history of repeated injuries and usurpations on the part of man toward woman, having in direct object the establishment of an absolute tyranny over her. To prove this, let facts be submitted to a candid world. . . . He has never permitted her to exercise her inalienable right to the elective franchise . . . he has compelled her to submit to laws, in the formation of which she had no voice . . . he has made her, if married, in the eyes of the law, civilly dead.[9]

It was a stroke of genius. The document elevated the women's struggle to the moral equivalent of the birth of the nation itself. In so doing, the delegates at Seneca Falls were challenging the patriotic devotion of the American male to the fundamental liberties articulated by the Declaration of Independence. To avoid any misunderstanding, the delegates attached to their document a list of resolutions demanding specific social and legal changes, including a role in lawmaking, improved property rights, equity in divorce, and access to education and the professions. All of the resolutions passed unanimously except for a demand to vote, something that was still considered too radical for many of the assembled delegates. By the 1890s, however, women's suffrage had become less threatening.

Not only was the movement better organized, but also more politically sophisticated. Suffragists became less threatening to men, who associated suffrage with divorce, promiscuity, and the neglect of children. Instead, suffragists claimed that because women occupied a distinct sphere from men—as mothers, wives, and homemakers—they would bring a special sensitivity to public life. Once women had the vote, they argued, intemperance would be drastically reduced and war would be eliminated since women would, by their calming influence, tame the belligerence of men. Tubman was enlisted by the National American Women Suffrage Association (NAWSA) to further the cause.[10]

Harriet had been encouraged to join the women's rights movement by her friends Martha Coffin Wright and Emily Howland, who were close allies of Susan B. Anthony and Elizabeth Cady Stanton, the most noted leaders of the NAWSA during this time.[11] Anthony and Stanton were eager to enlist prominent black women into the movement and had already succeeded with Frances Watkins Harper and Sojourner Truth. Harper, a well-educated, freeborn African American woman, was an accomplished poet and writer who represented an ideal of middle-class black womanhood. Truth, on the other hand, was born a slave in upstate New York in 1797. Originally named Isabella Baumfree, she was freed in 1826 and changed her name to Sojourner Truth after being called to spread God's word as an itinerant preacher. Truth was a riveting speaker who once bared her breasts during a public suffrage meeting when pro-slavery hecklers doubted she was a woman. She used the incident to defend her womanhood while also denigrating the manhood of her critics. Truth also shocked proper society by attempting to vote in Battle Creek, Michigan, in the early 1870s.[12] Although Harper and Truth were the most highly visible African-American feminists in the country, Harriet provided a refreshing contrast for the movement. Unlike Harper, she was an illiterate former slave whose life had been exploited by the emotional and physical abuse of white men. As a result, she could speak to the circumstances of millions of former slave women. Unlike Truth, Harriet embraced an identity that crossed gender lines. She was proud of her military prowess and experience as well as her leadership abilities, qualities that were associated with white masculinity in the 19th century. As a result, her deeds as an Underground Railroad conductor and Civil War nurse and scout made her equal to any man who questioned her worth. That fact was not lost on the local press. When Harriet spoke before the Non-Partisan Society of Political Education for Women in Auburn in March 1888, she received very favorable coverage:

> In view of Mrs. Tubman's services in the late war, in freeing and helping to emancipate her down trodden and oppressed race, the

ladies of the society requested that she say a few words before the society. . . . Her recital of the brave and fearless deeds of women who sacrificed all for their country and moved in battle when bullets mowed down men, file after file, and rank after rank, was graphic. Loving women were on the scene to administer to the injured, to bind up their wounds and tend them through weary months of suffering in the army hospitals. If those deeds do not place them as man's equal, what do? The speaker said that her prayers carried her through and they would eventually place woman at the ballot box with man, as his equal. Her speech, though brief, was very interesting, and was listened to with rapt attention by all.[13]

Tubman also traveled to New York, Boston, and Washington, D.C., to speak in favor of women's voting rights. She described her actions during and after the Civil War, and used the sacrifices of countless women throughout modern history as evidence of women's equality to men.[14] Once, when asked whether she believed women ought to have the vote, Harriet replied: "I suffered enough to believe it."[15] During these appearances Tubman inspired a new generation of feminist leaders who had benefited from the establishment of colleges for black women as well as from church-related work. Employing grassroots activism, this younger generation learned from successes of such national organizations as the Women's Christian Temperance Movement and the white women's club movement, and founded an organization of its own—the National Association of Colored Women. The NACW was dedicated to uplifting the black race by placing moral and political pressure on the elite white community to change its exclusionary policies. In addition, the organization was involved in social service work at the local and regional levels. Tubman was quickly embraced by the organization as an "inspiration for the rising generation of colored women."[16]

During this hectic period of her life, Harriet always returned home to Auburn, where she found solace in the company of her family and an ongoing purpose in caring for the elderly blacks she took in. Nelson was especially supportive, though his tuberculosis had taken a severe toll physically. On October 18, 1888, he succumbed to the disease. He was just 45 years old.[17] Harriet was devastated by the loss, but continued

I Sell the Shadow to Support the Substance.
SOJOURNER TRUTH.

Sojourner Truth, ca. 1875. Born a slave, Truth (ca. 1797–1883) was freed by New York State law in 1827, although she had already claimed her freedom. She became an articulate crusader for abolitionism and women's rights. (Courtesy of the Library of Congress)

to find purpose in her work for women's rights and the dream of John Brown Hall.

In 1896, Tubman served as the keynote speaker at the founding convention of the NACW at Washington, D.C., and was given a standing ovation by the audience. Hailed as "Mother Tubman" in a subsequent speech by Rosetta Douglass-Sprague, the daughter of Frederick Douglass, Harriet's example was used to inspire club members to build new social institutions "for the betterment of the condition of their brothers and sisters."[18]

Viewed in the broader context of the Progressive Era, the appeal was an especially powerful one. Beginning in the 1880s, white urban middle-class women became deeply concerned with the problems associated with industrialization and rapid urbanization. Appalled by the decline in quality of life within cities, they began to fight for social justice, concentrating on ending poverty, prostitution, and juvenile delinquency. Most of these female reformers were first–generation college graduates who ignored traditional social norms and worked outside the home as schoolteachers, librarians, business clerks, and typists. Participating in reform organizations was a way to perform public service and also have a job. As a result, white women established such reform institutions as settlement houses, or safe residences in poor neighborhoods where they could study local conditions. Their example motivated African American women to join with their white counterparts in reform societies like the Women's Christian Temperance Union and also organize institutions of their own. Tubman seized the opportunity to promote John Brown Hall.

By the mid-1890s, Harriet realized that her income, even when supplemented by donations from white benefactors, would never allow her to finance a fully subsidized nursing home for elderly black women. While she sought to divest herself of financial management, she did not want to surrender her control over the development of the institution. Harriet considered donating her property and home to either the A.M.E. Zion Church or the NACW in the hope that one of those institutions would bring her dream to fruition. Although the NACW expressed a desire to help raise funding for the project, it declined the offer, not wanting to accept complete financial responsibility for it. Instead, Harriet turned to the church. In 1896, the bishop of the A.M.E. Zion Western New York Conference agreed to assume the mortgage on the land for the John Brown Hall, though the official transfer of the property would not occur until 1903. The conference also agreed to raise funds for the project.[19] Harriet made the agreement on the stipulation that the facility be made into a home for "aged and indigent colored people."[20]

Shortly after the property was transferred in 1903, differences arose between church officials and Harriet's white friends. The latter group was opposed to church control of the property, believing that Harriet would have no equity in the property and would become destitute.

The Reverend B. F. Wheeler, the first A.M.E. Zion supervisor of the property, assured them that Harriet was "to have a life interest in all money accruing from rents, on the condition that she pay the taxes and keep up the insurance."[21] Of greater concern to Harriet's white associates was the addition to the property of a "school of domestic science where [black] girls may be taught the various branches of industrial education." According to Wheeler, the A.M.E. Church was prepared to make this concession as well:

The public are in great sympathy with the [creation] of John Brown
Hall, and if the General conference can arrange to let the super-
intendent give his whole time to the work, this home will soon
be developed into a great institution for aged and infirm colored
people, who are constantly seeking shelter under its roof. . . . The
deed conveying the property to the church stipulates that when
the trustees see their way clear to do so, they shall establish on the
ground beside the home, a school of domestic science where girls
may be taught the various branches on industrial education. This
feature of the work is particularly popular with the white people in
this western part of the state of New York.[22]

The inclusion of a school of domestic science reflected the significant
difference of opinion among blacks. Some African American leaders like
Booker T. Washington, a former slave who founded the Tuskegee Institute in Alabama, advocated industrial education for blacks as a means
of gaining respect and entry into the white mainstream. Whites whole-
heartedly agreed with this position and patronized industrial schools for
blacks.[23] Others, like W.E.B. Du Bois, a Harvard-educated sociologist,
discouraged such an accomodationist perspective, believing that industrial education could only served to "keep the black race down." Du Bois
insisted that blacks must also be given the opportunity for an academic
education if they were ever to compete economically in white society.[24]
Still others, like Rosetta Douglass-Sprague, believed that industrial train-
ing was a "first step" in a much larger process of racial uplift that would
eventually lead to higher education for blacks.[25] Accordingly, there was
a division of opinion among Harriet's white and black friends over the
nature of the school to be established. If Harriet herself had a preference,
there is no written record of it. Instead, she gave her full support to fundraising efforts for the "Harriet Tubman Home," as it was referred to in the
newspapers by 1904.[26]

Fundraising was done almost exclusively by Harriet's white friends
and a board of women from the A.M.E. Zion Church. The church's regional conference also established an annual collection with a target
goal of $200 for the maintenance of the five-bedroom facility after it
was completed in 1908.[27] Despite the fundraising efforts—and Harriet's
membership on the board of trustees—the church ordered residents to

pay a $100 entrance fee. Harriet was dismayed when she learned of the policy. "They make a rule that nobody should come in without having a hundred dollars," she complained. "I wanted to make a rule that nobody should come in unless they didn't have no money at all."[28] Still, she agreed to be the guest of honor when the Harriet Tubman Home for the Aged opened on June 23, 1908. According to the Auburn newspapers, the legendary Underground Railroad conductor expressed confidence that others would continue her mission in the future:

> With stars and stripes wound about her shoulders, a band playing national airs and a concourse of members of her race gathered about her to pay tribute to her lifetime struggle in behalf of the colored people, aged Harriet Tubman Davis, the Moses of her people, yesterday experienced one of the Happiest days of her life . . .
>
> When called upon by the chairman for a few words of welcome, the aged woman stated that she had but started the work for the rising generation to take up. "I did not take up this work for my own benefit," said she, "but for those of my race who need help. The work is now well started and I know God will raise up others to take care of the future. All I ask is united effort, for 'united we stand, divided we fall.'"[29]

Harriet's plea for a "united effort" was a reference to the difference of opinion between her white friends and the church over plans for an industrial school, as well as her disappointment that the church was charging a fee for admission into the nursing home.

By 1910, Harriet, who was nearly 90 years old, had lost the use of her legs and spent most of her time in a wheelchair. The sleeping spells and headaches from her childhood head trauma continued to afflict her. Unable to sleep because of the pains and "buzzing" in her head, she asked a doctor if he could operate and underwent brain surgery at Boston's Massachusetts General Hospital. Refusing anesthesia, Harriet reportedly chose instead to bite down on a bullet, as she had seen Civil War soldiers do when their limbs were amputated.[30] According to Harriet, the operation was a success, since her "head [felt] more comfortable later on."[31]

One of the few enjoyments Harriet experienced during the last years of her life were visits by her family and friends. Her young

Harriet Tubman in old age, ca. 1912. (Courtesy of
the Library of Congress)

niece, Alice Brickler, recalled that she and her mother, Margaret
Stewart Lucas, would often visit Tubman, bringing her "sweets,
which she liked so well."

Nevertheless, by 1911, Harriet's body was so frail that she was forced
to move into the home that bore her name. Described as "ill and pen-
niless" by one newspaper, she struggled to pay the cost of her private
nursing care, which was $10 per week. Supporters offered a new round
of donations and also wrote appeals for donations to private individuals, reform organizations, and newspapers.[32] In November 1912, Harriet
prepared a will, naming three women as heirs: Mary Gaston, a niece;
Katy Stewart, a grandniece; and Frances Smith, the matron of the Harriet Tubman Home. The three women would eventually inherit Harriet's
private home and its seven acres.[33] She had outlived most of her siblings,
two husbands, and even some of her nieces and nephews. But old age

had robbed her of good health and personal dignity and she was ready to die.

Surrounded by friends and family members, Harriet Tubman died of pneumonia on the evening of March 10, 1913. Just before she passed away, she told those who had gathered in the room: "I go to prepare a place for you."[34]

On the afternoon of March 13, hundreds of mourners flocked to Thompson Memorial A.M.E. Zion Church in Auburn to view her body and pay their last respects. After a final service, Tubman's flag-draped coffin was removed to nearby Fort Hill Cemetery, where she was buried with military honors.[35]

NOTES

1. Ward O'Hara, ed., *Auburn, NY: Two Hundred Years of History, 1793–1993* (Auburn, NY: Auburn Bicentennial Committee, 1992), 23.

2. Jean Humez, *Harriet Tubman: The Life and the Life Stories* (Madison: University of Wisconsin, 2003), 92.

3. Reverend James E. Mason, "Tribute to Harriet Tubman" (June 6, 1914). Harriet Tubman Home, Auburn, New York.

4. See Rosa Belle Holt, "A Heroine in Ebony," *Chautauquan* 23 (July 1896): 460; and Lillie Wyman, "Harriet Tubman," *New England Magazine* 6 (March 1896): 116.

5. Tubman, quoted in Sarah Bradford, *Harriet, the Moses of Her People*, rev. ed. (New York: J. J. Little, 1901), 149–150.

6. Kate Clifford Larson, *Bound for the Promised Land: Harriet Tubman, Portrait of an American Hero* (New York: Ballantine Books, 2004), 264, 271.

7. Aileen S. Kraditor, *Means and Ends in American Abolitionism: Garrison and His Critics on Strategy and Tactics, 1834–1850* (New York: Vintage, 1970, paperback), 39–77; and Julie Roy Jeffrey, *The Great Silent Army of Abolitionism: Ordinary Women in the Antislavery Movement* (Chapel Hill: University of North Carolina, 1998).).

8. Ronald G. Walters, *American Reformers, 1815–1860* (New York: Hill & Wang, 1978, paperback), 104–112.

9. "Declaration of Sentiments," July 20, 1848, quoted in Margaret Hope Bacon, *Valiant Friend: The Life of Lucretia Mott* (New York: Walker, 1980), 127.

10. Rosalyn Terborg-Penn, *African-American Women in the Struggle for the Vote, 1850–1920* (Bloomington: Indiana University Press, 1998), 40–41.

11. Humez, *Harriet Tubman*, 97.

12. See Kate Clifford Larson, *Bound for the Promised Land: Harriet Tubman, Portrait of an American Hero* (New York: Ballantine Books, 2004),168, 254; Olive Gilbert, *Narrative of Sojourner Truth*, ed. William Kaufman (Mineola, NY: Dover, 1997), iii–vi; and Terborg-Penn, *African-American Women in Struggle for Vote*, 40–41.

13. "Suffragists," *Auburn (NY) Morning Dispatch:* March 16, 1888.

14. Larson, *Bound for the Promised Land*, 273.

15. Tubman, quoted in Catherine Clinton, *Harriet Tubman: The Road to Freedom* (New York: Little, Brown, 2004), 191.

16. Victoria Earle, "Harriet Tubman," (Boston) *Woman's Era* (June 1896): 8.

17. See Harriet Tubman, "Affidavit Testimony in Pension Claim Case" (November 10, 1894), Cayuga County Clerk's Office, Auburn, New York.

18. Rosetta Douglass-Sprague, quoted in "Minutes of July 20, 1896," *Official Minutes of the National Federation of Afro-American Women Held in Washington, D.C.* (Washington, D.C.: National Association of Colored Women's Clubs, 1902): 36.

19. Humez, *Harriet Tubman*, 102–103.

20. Tubman, quoted in Clinton, *Road to Freedom*, 209.

21. "Minutes, Twenty-Second Quadrenniel Session, A.M.E. Zion General Conference, 1904," quoted in William J. Walls, *The African-Methodist Episcopal Zion Church* (Charlotte, NC: A.M.E. Zion Church, 1974), 439–444.

22. Walls, "Minutes."

23. John Hope Franklin, *From Slavery to Freedom: A History of Negro Americans*, 5th ed. (New York: Knopf, 1980), 275–276.

24. William C. Kashatus, "'To Be Both A Negro and An American': W.E.B. Du Bois and His Search for an African American Identity," *Pennsylvania Heritage* 27, no. 2 (Spring 2001): 6–13.

25. Douglass-Sprague, "Minutes of July 1896," 36.

26. See *Auburn (NY) Daily Advertiser:* June 20, 1903, June 16, 1904, and June 14, 1907.

27. Humez, *Harriet Tubman*, 105.

28. Tubman quoted in Larson, *Bound for the Promised Land*, 285.

29. Tubman quoted in "Tubman Home Open," *Auburn (NY) Daily Advertiser:* June 24, 1908.

30. Larson, *Bound for the Promised Land*, 282.

31. Tubman quoted in Larson, *Bound for the Promised Land*, 282.

32. Larson, *Bound for the Promised Land*, 288.

33. Clinton, *Road to Freedom*, 213.

34. Tubman, quoted in Clinton, *Road to Freedom*, 214.

35. Larson, *Bound for the Promised Land*, 289.

Chapter 9

LEGACY

Harriet Tubman became an American icon in the years after she died. But there was a distinct difference of opinion over the meaning of her life and labors. Some viewed Tubman as the penultimate example of a law-abiding African American citizen. The City of Auburn, for example, commemorated her life with a bronze plaque on the courthouse listing her many achievements. The tablet was dedicated on June 12, 1914, with a public ceremony that recognized Tubman's contributions to humanity. Booker T. Washington delivered the keynote address, recognizing her as a role model, especially for law-abiding black people:

> In her simplicity, her modesty, her common sense, her devotion to duty, she has left for us an example which those in the present generation of all races might strive to emulate. In the tens of millions of black people scattered throughout this country there are many great souls, heroic souls, that the white race does not know about. Harriet Tubman brought the two races together and made it possible for the white race to know the black race, to place a different estimate on it. In too many sections of our country the white man knows the criminal Negro, but he knows little about

the law-abiding Negro; he knows much of the worst types of our race, he does not know enough of the best types of our race.[1]

While Washington used Tubman to justify his accommodationist philosophy, Harriet represented a more militant perspective in the African American experience. Unlike Washington, who deferred to the white mainstream, Tubman challenged the white power structure throughout her life.

As an Underground Railroad conductor, Harriet repeatedly violated federal law to free those in bondage and defended her illegal activities by embracing God's higher law over unjust civil measures. By the 1860s, she was as revered in the North for her abolitionist activities as she was vilified in the South for violating the Fugitive Slave Law. In the process, Tubman condoned violence by threatening to shoot fugitives who succumbed to fear and exhaustion on the journey north, and by assisting the radical abolitionist John Brown in his plans to lead a bloody slave insurrection. Like Brown, she viewed slavery as a state of war, and his death galvanized her commitment to emancipation regardless of the consequences. Accordingly, Tubman's role as a scout during the Civil War was also consistent with her belief that the end of emancipation justified whatever means were necessary to achieve it. In all these involvements, Tubman proved herself to be a person of action, rather than words. She understood that the spoken word may be inspirational, but unless supported by direct action, it was meaningless.

This militant approach was unique among females of the time period and earned Tubman the respect and admiration of males, both black and white, who referred to her as "General" and the "Moses of Her People." At the same time, Harriet's self-initiative and independence appealed to a growing women's rights movement, which enlisted her for their cause near the end of her life. While some reformers identified a contradiction between the two roles, others celebrated Harriet as a civil rights pioneer. She never seemed to view herself as anything more than an instrument of God's will. Nevertheless, Harriet Tubman was embraced by several groups who adapted her example to meet their own special cause.

During the 1920s, the African American community kept her memory alive in juvenile literature on black heroes and heroines, and ladies' auxiliaries of the A.M.E. Zion Church formed Harriet Tubman clubs.

Historian James A. McGowan (1932–2008) inspired
renewed interest in Harriet Tubman during the 1990s
through an online journal that served as an indispensable
reference for scholars. (Courtesy of the Estate of
James A. McGowan)

In the 1930s, Tubman was used by the American communist movement as a feminist icon. Their objective was to promote unionization
among black women.[2] One communist sympathizer, Earl Conrad, a former Teamster Union organizer in Harlem, began researching a new biography of Tubman in 1938. Conrad wrote in an academic style and his
work was much better researched than Bradford's earlier treatments.
Instead of mythologizing Tubman, he aimed to document the historical
importance of her life for scholars and the nation's memory. But Conrad experienced great difficulty finding a publisher and endured con-
tempt for his efforts to construct a more objective, detailed account of
Tubman's life for adults. The book, titled *Harriet Tubman: Negro Soldier
and Abolitionist*, was finally published by Carter G. Woodson's Associated Publishers in 1942.[3]

Despite the criticism, Conrad's biography sparked public interest in Tubman and the Underground Railroad. To address the interest, Bishop W. J. Walls of the African Methodist Episcopal Church's Western New York Conference proposed that the Harriet Tubman Home for the Aged be restored as a memorial to the legendary civil rights pioneer. The facility was vacated in 1920 when its last resident died, and it stood empty for the next two decades, falling into disrepair. In 1944, Bishop Wall raised $2,500 to begin the restoration process; the remaining $31,000 was contributed by A.M.E. churches in New York, New England, and North Carolina. Completely restored by 1949, the Harriet Tubman Home was dedicated on April 13, 1953, and opened to the public shortly after.[4]

Tubman was celebrated in many other ways as well. Dozens of schools and streets were named in her honor. In 1937, the Empire State Federation of Women's Clubs erected a tombstone over her grave at Fort Hill Cemetery in Auburn to celebrate her accomplishments. In 1944, the United States Maritime Commission launched the SS *Harriet Tubman*, its first Liberty ship ever named for a black woman. Black artists also celebrated Tubman's legacy. Between 1939 and 1940, Jacob Lawrence created a 31-panel series of paintings depicting various scenes from her life. Another treatment completed by William H. Johnson in 1945 shows Tubman in soldier's garb and is in the collection of the Smithsonian American Art Museum in Washington, D.C.[5] In 1978, the United States Postal Service issued a stamp in honor of Tubman as the first in a series honoring African Americans.[6] In the 1990s, recreational parks in Boston, Cambridge, Maryland, and Wilmington, Delaware, were dedicated in Tubman's honor. A survey at the end of the 20th century named Harriet as one of the most famous civilians in American history before the Civil War and she continues to be commemorated together with Elizabeth Cady Stanton, Amelia Bloomer, and Sojourner Truth in the calendar of saints of the Episcopal Church on July 20.[7]

Despite Tubman's significance, most historians deferred to Earl Conrad's 1942 biography as the seminal work on her life until the 1990s, when President Bill Clinton initiated a national dialogue on race. The initiative resulted in a renewed interest in the Underground Railroad in general, and Harriet Tubman in particular. Historian James McGowan seized the opportunity to publish *The Harriet Tubman Journal* as a vehicle to rescue Tubman from all the inconsistencies, exaggerations, and distortions that had been imposed upon her in books, artwork, and films down through the generations. The periodical, which also appeared on the Internet, quickly became a valuable reference for scholars, researchers, and writers.

Within the next decade, three new biographies of Tubman appeared: Jean M. Humez's *Harriet Tubman: The Life and Life Stories* (2003); Catherine Clinton's *Harriet Tubman: The Road to Freedom* (2004); and Kate Clifford Larson's *Bound for the Promised Land: Harriet Tubman, Portrait of an American Hero* (2004). Of the three works, Larson's is the most informative and groundbreaking, going so far as to identify the names of the fugitives rescued by Tubman on specific missions. But all three biographies offer a more human portrait of this American icon while tapping into the enduring myth that with hard work and persistence, anyone can rise above their humble origins to achieve greatness. It is that struggle and ultimate success against adversity that make Harriet Tubman the continuing source of inspiration that she is today and will remain for generations to come.

NOTES

1. Booker T. Washington, "Extracts from an Address at the Unveiling of the Harriet Tubman Memorial," quoted in Louis R. Harlan and Raymond W. Smock, eds., *The Booker T. Washington Papers* (New York: Oxford University Press, 1980), 13:59–60.

2. Kate Clifford Larson, *Bound for the Promised Land: Harriet Tubman, Portrait of an American Hero* (New York: Ballantine Books, 2004), 291–294.

3. Larson, *Bound for the Promised Land*, 294.

4. See African Methodist Episcopal Zion Church, "Program of the Dedication of the Harriet Tubman Home, Auburn, New York," April 13, 1953. Manuscript Collection, Cornell University Library, Ithaca, New York.

5. Catherine Clinton, "Slavery Is War: Harriet Tubman and the Underground Railroad," in *Passage to Freedom: The Underground Railroad in*

History and Memory, ed. David W. Blight (Washington, D.C.: Smithsonian Institute, 2004), 209.

6. U.S. Postal Service, "Postal Service Celebrates 25th Anniversary of Black Heritage Stamp Series," February 21, 2002. Online at USPS Newsroom.

7. Larson, *Bound for the Promised Land*, xv–xx; Clinton, *Road to Freedom*, 215–216.

SELECTED BIBLIOGRAPHY

"A Colored Man Murdered." *Baltimore American:* October 7, 1867.

"Acquittal of Murderer." *Baltimore American:* December 23, 1867.

African Methodist Episcopal Zion Church. "Program of the Dedication of the Harriet Tubman Home, Auburn, New York," April 13, 1953. Manuscript Collection, Cornell University Library, Ithaca, New York.

Bacon, Margaret H. *Valiant Friend: The Life of Lucretia Mott.* New York: Walker and Company, 1980.

Berlin, Ira. "The Structure of the Free Negro Caste in the Antebellum United States." *Journal of Social History* 9 (Spring 1976): 305–311.

Blassingame, John W. *The Slave Community: Plantation Life in the Antebellum South.* New York: Oxford University, 1978 (paperback edition).

Blight, David W., ed. *Passage to Freedom: The Underground Railroad in History and Memory.* Washington, D.C.: Smithsonian Institute, 2004.

Blockson, Charles L. *African Americans in Pennsylvania.* Baltimore: Black Classics, 1994.

Blockson, Charles L. "Escape from Slavery: The Underground Railroad." *National Geographic* (July 1984): 39–46.

Blockson, Charles L. *Hippocrene Guide to the Underground Railroad*. New York: Hippocrene Books, 1994.

Bordewich, Fergus M. *Bound for Canaan: The Underground Railroad and the War for the Soul of America*. New York: Amistad, 2005.

Borome, Joseph A. "The Vigilant Committee of Philadelphia." *Pennsylvania Magazine of History and Biography*, 92 (July 1968): 320–351.

Bradford, Sarah H. *Harriet Tubman: The Moses of Her People*. 1886. Reprint, Secaucus, NJ: Citadel Press, 1961.

Bradford, Sarah H. *Scenes in the Life of Harriet Tubman*. Auburn, NY: W. J. Moses, 1869.

Brickler, Alice H. Letter to Earl Conrad: July 28, 1939. Earl Conrad / Harriet Tubman Collection. Schomburg Center for Research in Black Culture, New York Public Library.

Brown, William W. *The Rising Son*. Boston: A. G. Brown, 1874.

Cameron, Kenneth, W., ed. *Correspondence of Franklin B. Sanborn the Transcendentalist*. Hartford, CT: Transcendental Books, 1982.

Campbell, Stanley. *The Slave Catchers: Enforcement of the Fugitive Slave Law, 1850–1860*. Chapel Hill: University of North Carolina, 1968.

Chadwick, Bruce. *Traveling the Underground Railroad*. Secaucus, NJ: Citadel Press, 1999.

Chaitin, Peter W. *The American Civil War: The Coastal War from Chesapeake Bay to Rio Grande*. Alexandria, VA: Time-Life Books, 1984.

Cheney, Ednah D. "Moses." *Freedmen's Record* (March 1865): 34–38.

Christianson, Scott. "The Battle for Charles Nalle." *American Legacy* 2 (Winter 1997): 31–35.

Clinton, Catherine. *Harriet Tubman: The Road to Freedom*. New York: Little, Brown, 2004.

Conrad, Earl. *Harriet Tubman: Negro Soldier and Abolitionist*. New York: International, 1942.

Courlander, Harold. *Negro Folk Music, U.S.A.* New York: Dover, 1992.

Davis, F. James. *Who Is Black? One Nation's Definition*. University Park, PA: Penn State Press, 1991.

"Death of Aunt Harriet, Moses of Her People." *Auburn Daily Advertiser:* March 11, 1913.

Donald, David H. *Lincoln.* New York: Simon & Schuster, 1996.

Douglass, Frederick. *The Life and Times of Frederick Douglass* (1881). Reprint, London: Collier Macmillan, 1969.

Douglass, Frederick. *The Life and Times of Frederick Douglass.* New York: Library Classics, 1994.

Douglass-Sprague, Rosetta. "Minutes of July 20, 1896." *Official Minutes of the National Federation of Afro-American Women Held in Washington, D.C.* Washington, D.C.: National Association of Colored Women's Clubs, 1902, 36.

Drake, Thomas E. *Quakers and Slavery in America.* New Haven: Yale University, 1950.

Drew, Benjamin. *The Refugee: A North-Side View of Slavery* (1855) Reprint, edited by Tilden G. Edelstein. Reading MA: Addison-Wesley Publishing Company, 1969.

Du Bois, W.E.B. *John Brown.* Philadelphia: George W. Jacobs & Company, 1909.

Dundes, Alan. "'Jumping the Broom': On the Origin and Meaning of an African American Wedding Custom." *Journal of American Folklore* (1996): 324–336.

Earle, Victoria. "Harriet Tubman." (Boston) *Woman's Era* (June 1896): 8.

Emilio, Luis F. *A Brave Black Regiment. History of the 54th Massachusetts Regiment.* 1894. Reprint, Salem, NH: Ayer, 1990.

Fehrenbacher, Don E., ed. *Abraham Lincoln: Speeches and Writings, 1859–1865.* 2 vols. New York: Library of America, 1989.

Fisher, Miles M. *Negro Slaves Songs in the United States.* New York: Citadel, 1968.

Floyd, Samuel A., Jr. *The Power of Black Music.* New York: Oxford University, 1995.

Foner, Eric. *Free Soil, Free Labor, Free Men: The Ideology of the Republican Party before the Civil War.* New York: Oxford University Press, 1970.

Foner, Eric. *Reconstruction: America's Unfinished Revolution, 1863–1877.* New York: Harper & Row, 1988.

Forbes, Ella. *But We Have No Country: The 1851 Christiana Resistance*. Cherry Hill, NJ: Africana Homestead Legacy Publishers, 1998.

Franklin, John Hope. *The Emancipation Proclamation*. New York: Doubleday, 1963.

Franklin, John Hope. *From Slavery to Freedom: A History of Negro Americans*, 5th ed. New York: Knopf, 1980.

Franklin, John Hope, and Loren Schweninger. *Runaway Slaves: Rebels on the Plantation*. New York: Oxford University Press, 1999.

"Fugitive Slave Rescue." *Troy Whig*: April 28, 1860.

Gara, Larry. *The Liberty Line: The Legend of the Underground Railroad*. Lexington: University of Kentucky, 1961.

Gates, Hernry L. *Lincoln on Race & Slavery*. Princeton, NJ: Princeton University Press, 2009.

Gatewood, Willard B. *Aristocrats of Color: The Black Elite, 1880–1920*. Bloomington: Indiana University Press, 1990.

Genovese, Eugene. *Roll Jordan, Roll: The World the Slaveholders Made*. New York: Pantheon, 1974.

Gilbert, Oliver. *Narrative of Sojourner Truth*, edited by William Kaufman. Mineola, NY: Dover, 1997.

Harlan, Louis R. and Raymond W. Smock, eds. *The Booker T. Washington Papers*. New York: Oxford University Press, 1980.

"Harriet Tubman." *American Magazine* 74 (1912): 420–422.

"Harriet Tubman." *Boston Herald*: October 31, 1886.

Harris, Kim and Reggie Harris. *Music and the Underground Railroad*. Philadelphia: Ascension, 1984.

Higginson, Mary T., ed. *Letters and Journals of Thomas Wentworth Higginson, 1846–1906*. New York: Negro Universities Press, 1906.

Holt, Rosa Belle. "A Heroine in Ebony." *Chautauquan* 23 (July 1896): 459–462.

Horton, James Oliver. *Free People of Color: Inside the African American Community*. Washington, D.C.: Smithsonian Institute, 1993.

Horton, James Oliver, and Lois E. Horton. *In Hope of Liberty: Culture, Community and Protest Among Northern Free Blacks, 1700–1860*. New York: Oxford University Press, 1997.

Horton, James Oliver, and Lois E. Horton. *Slavery and the Making of America*. New York: Oxford University Press, 2005.

Humez, Jean. *Harriet Tubman: The Life and the Life Stories*. Madison: University of Wisconsin, 2003.

Jeffrey, Julie Roy. *The Great Silent Army of Abolitionism: Ordinary Women in the Antislavery Movement*. Chapel Hill: University of North Carolina, 1998.

Jones, Arthur C. *Wade in the Water: The Wisdom of the Spirituals*. New York: Orbis, 1993.

Jordan, Ryan P. *Slavery and the Meetinghouse: The Quakers and the Abolitionist Dilemma, 1820–1865*. Bloomington: Indiana University, 2007.

Kashatus, William C. *Just Over the Line: Chester County and the Underground Railroad*. University Park, PA: Penn State Press, 2002.

Kashatus, William C. "'To Be Both A Negro and An American': W.E.B. DuBois and His Search for an African American Identity." *Pennsylvania Heritage* 27, no. 2 (Spring 2001): 6–13.

Kashatus, William C. *In Pursuit of Freedom: Teaching the Underground Railroad*. Portsmouth, NH: Heinemann, 2005.

Kolchin, Peter. *American Slavery, 1619–1877*. New York: Hill & Wang, 1993.

Kraditor, Aileen S. *Means and Ends in American Abolitionism: Garrison and His Critics on Strategy and Tactics, 1834–1850*. New York: Vintage, 1970.

Larson, Kate Clifford. *Bound for the Promised Land: Harriet Tubman, Portrait of an American Hero*. New York: Ballantine Books, 2004.

Levine, Bruce. *Half Slave and Half Free: The Roots of the Civil War*. New York: Hill & Wang, 1992.

Marietta, Jack. *The Reformation of American Quakerism, 1748–1783*. Philadelphia: University of Pennsylvania Press, 1984.

Mason, Reverend James E. "Tribute to Harriet Tubman." (June 6, 1914). Harriet Tubman Home, Auburn, New York.

McDaniel, Donna and Vanessa Julye. *Fit for Freedom, Not for Friendship: Quakers, African Americans, and the Myth of Racial Justice*. Philadelphia: Quaker Press, 2009.

McGowan, James A. "The Psychic Life of Harriet Tubman." *Visions Magazine* (March 1995): 1–3.

McGowan, James A. *Station Master on the Underground Railroad: The Life and Letters of Thomas Garrett*. Jefferson, NC: McFarland, 2005.

McGowan, James A., ed. *Harriet Tubman Journal*, 1993–2007.

McGowan, James A., and William C. Kashatus. *Angel at Philadelphia: A Study of William Still's Underground Railroad*. Unpublished manuscript. 2010.

McPherson, James M. *Abraham Lincoln and the Second American Revolution*. New York: Oxford, 1990.

McPherson, James M. *The Negro's Civil War: How American Negroes Felt and Acted During the War for the Union*. New York: Ballantine Books, 1991.

"Moses of the Negroes." *Literary Digest* 46 (1912): 913–916.

Mowbray, Calvin W., and Maurice D. Rimpo. *Close-ups of Early Dorchester County History*. Silver Spring, MD: Family Line Publications, 1988.

Nash, Gary B. *Forging Freedom: The Formation of Philadelphia's Black Community, 1720–1840*. Cambridge, MA: Harvard University, 1988.

Nash, Gary B., and Jean R. Soderlund. *Freedom By Degrees: Emancipation in Pennsylvania and Its Aftermath*. New York: Oxford University Press, 1991.

Neeley, Mark E., Jr. *The Fate of Liberty: Abraham Lincoln and Civil Liberties*. New York: Oxford University, 1991.

Oates, Stephen B. *To Purge This Land with Blood: A Biography of John Brown*. Amherst: University of Massachusetts, 1984.

O'Hara, Ward, ed. *Auburn, NY: Two Hundred Years of History, 1793–1993*. Auburn, NY: Auburn Bicentennial Committee, 1992.

Osgood, Lucy. Letter to Lydia Maria Child, June 2, 1859. Lydia Maria Child Papers, Cornell University Library, Ithaca, New York.

Pennsylvania Yearly Meeting of Progressive Friends. *Proceedings* (1853). Chester County Historical Society, West Chester, Pennsylvania.

Potter, David M. *The Impending Crisis, 1848–1861*. New York: Harper & Row, 1976.

Quarles, Benjamin. *Black Abolitionists*. New York: Da Capo Press, 1969 (paperback edition).

Quarles, Benjamin. *The Negro in the Civil War*. New York: Da Capo Press, 1989 (paperback edition).

Renehan, Edward J., Jr. *The Secret Six: The True Tale of the Men Who Conspired with John Brown*. New York: Crown, 1995.

Reynolds, David S. *John Brown, Abolitionist: The Man Who Killed Slavery, Sparked the Civil War, and Seeded Civil Rights*. New York: Knopf, 2006.

Ripley, C. Peter. *Underground Railroad*. Washington, D.C.: United States Department of the Interior, 1998.

Robinson, John B. *Pictures of Slavery and Anti-Slavery* (1863). Reprint, Miami, FL: Mnemosyne Publishing, 1969.

Sanborn, Franklin B. "Harriet Tubman." *Boston Commonwealth:* July 17, 1863.

Sanborn, Frederick B., ed. *The Life and Letters of John Brown*. New York: Negro Universities, 1885.

Sernett, Milton C. *Harriet Tubman: Myth, Memory, and History*. Durham, NC: Duke University Press, 2007.

Sernett, Milton C. *North Star Country: Upstate New York and the Crusade for African American Freedom*. Syracuse, NY: Syracuse University, 2002.

Siebert, Wilbur H. *The Underground Railroad: From Slavery to Freedom*. New York: Macmillan, 1898. Reprint, New York: Russell & Russell, 1967.

Slaughter, Thomas. *Bloody Dawn: The Christiana Riot and Racial Violence in the Antebellum North*. New York: Oxford University Press, 1991.

Smedley, Robert C. *History of the Underground Railroad in Chester and the Neighboring Counties of Pennsylvania* (1883). Reprinted by Arno Press, New York, 1969.

Soderlund, Jean R. *Quakers and Slavery: A Divided Spirit*. Princeton, NJ: Princeton University Press, 1985.

Stampp, Kenneth M. *The Era of Reconstruction, 1865–1877*. New York: Vintage, 1965 paperback.

Stampp, Kenneth M. *The Peculiar Institution: Slavery in the Antebellum South*. New York: Viking, 1956.

Sterling, Dorothy, ed. *We Are Your Sisters: Black Women in the Nineteenth Century*. New York: Norton, 1984.

Still, William. *Underground Railroad*. 1872. Reprint, Chicago: Johnson Publishing, 1970.

"Suffragists." *Auburn (NY) Morning Dispatch:* March 16, 1888.

Switala, William J. *Underground Railroad in Delaware, Maryland, and West Virginia.* Mechanicsburg, PA: Stackpole Books, 2004.

Switala, William J. *Underground Railroad in Pennsylvania.* Mechanicsburg, PA: Stackpole Books, 2001.

Tatlock, Helen. Letter to Earl Conrade: September 9, 1939. Earl Conrad / Harriet Tubman Collection, Schomburg Center for Research in Black Culture, New York Public Library.

Telford, Emma P. "Harriet: The Modern Moses of Heroism and Visions." Ca. 1905. Typescript. Cayuga County Museum, Auburn, New York.

Terborg-Penn, Rosalyn. *African-American Women in the Struggle for the Vote, 1850–1920.* Bloomington: Indiana University Press, 1998.

Tobin, Jacquline L. and Raymond G. Dobard. *Hidden in Plain View: A Secret Story of Quilts and the Underground Railroad.* New York: Anchor, 2000.

Tobin, Jacqueline L. and Hettie Jones. *From Midnight to Dawn: The Last Tracks of the Underground Railroad.* New York: Doubleday, 2007.

Tubman, Harriet. "Affidavit Testimony in Pension Claim Case." (November 10, 1894), Cayuga County Clerk's Office, Auburn, New York.

Tubman, Harriet. "Petition for Harriet Tubman." Filed with Harriet Tubman War Service Testimonial Materials, Records of the House of Representatives. National Archives and Records Administration, Washington, D.C.

"Tubman Home Open." *Auburn (NY) Daily Advertiser:* June 24, 1908.

U.S. Postal Service. "Postal Service Celebrates 25th Anniversary of Black Heritage Stamp Series." February 21, 2002. Online at USPS Newsroom. Date of access: January 12, 2010.

Wahl, Albert J. "The Congregational or Progressive Friends in the Pre-Civil War Reform Movement." (PhD dissertation, Temple University, 1951).

Walls, William J. *The African-Methodist Episcopal Zion Church.* Charlotte, NC: A.M.E. Zion Church, 1974.

Walls, William J. *Harriet Tubman.* Charlotte, NC: A.M.E. Zion Church, 1946.

Walters, Ronald G. *American Reformers, 1815–1860.* New York: Hill & Wang, 1978.

Wright, Martha Coffin. Letter to Marianne Pelham Mott: November 7, 1865. Garrison Family Papers, Sophia Smith Collection, Smith College, Northampton, Massachusetts.

Wright, Martha Coffin. Letter to Sisters: October 8, 1868. Garrison Family Papers, Sophia Smith Collection. Smith College, Northampton, Massachusetts.

Wyman, Lillie. "Harriet Tubman." *New England Magazine* (March 1896): 110–118.

INDEX

National Anti-Slavery Standard, 46

National Association of Colored Women (NACW), 136–37, 138

Negro spirituals, 23, 49–52

New York Anti-Slavery Society, 70–71

Niagara Falls Suspension Bridge, 38, 47, 71

North Star, 23, 52

North Star (Douglass), 37

Otwell, Thomas, 72–73

Parker, Theodore, 83

Parker, William, 39

Parrish, Anne, xv

Pattison, Atthow, 4, 20

Pennington, Peter, 69–71

Pennsylvania Anti-Slavery Society, 39–40, 60–61

Pennypacker, Elijah, 63

Perry, Rev. Samuel, 44

Philadelphia, Pennsylvania, 25–26, 30, 43–44, 52

Philadelphia Vigilance Committee, 25, 39–40, 55 n.18

Phillips, Wendell, 89

Port Royal, South Carolina, xiii, 100, 103

Post, Amy, 47

Post, Isaac, 47

Prado, Henry, 73

Quakers (Religious Society of Friends), 3, 23–24, 62–65;

antislavery beliefs of, 62–65; Progressive Friends, 63–65; theology of, 62–63

Reconstruction era, 114–17

Religious Society of Friends. *See* Quakers

Republican Party, 95–99, 114–16

Robinson, John Bell, 89–90

Ross, Benjamin Jr., 6, 21–22, 66, 74

Ross, Benjamin Sr., 4, 72–74, 87

Ross, Henry, 21–22, 66–67, 74

Ross, James, 74

Ross, Linah, 5, 20

Ross, Mariah, 5

Ross, Moses, 6

Ross, Rachel, 69, 90

Ross, Robert, 6, 66, 74

Ross, Sophie, 5, 20

Ross, William H., 74

Sanborn, Franklin B., xiii, 83, 100, 106

Scenes in the Life of Harriet Tubman (Bradford), xiv, 120–21

Second Great Awakening, 117

Seneca Falls Conference, 134

Seward, Francis Adeline, 45–46, 88

Seward, Senator William H., 45–46, 87, 88, 96, 103, 121

Shaw, Colonel Robert Gould, 105, 107

Shimer, Anthony, 125

Sims, Thomas, 39

Slavery, 6–8, 17–18; auctions, 28; caste system, 18–19, 31 n.11; inhumanity of, 7; profitability, 6; religion, 11; resistance, 7–8; skin color, 18–19, 31 n.9; weddings, 18
Smith, Frances, 141
Smith, Garrett, 46–47, 83, 117
Smith, Stephen, 43
South Carolina, 95–96
SS *Harriet Tubman* (Liberty ship), 148
St. Catharines, Canada, 38, 47, 74, 79, 83, 91
Stanton, Edwin M., 103, 104
Stanton, Elizabeth Cady, 133–34, 135, 148
Stearns, George L., 83
Stevens, Thaddeus, 39
Stewart, James A., 12
Stewart, John H., 124–25, 126
Stewart, Katy, 141
Stewart, Margaret. *See* Tubman, Margaret
Stewart, William H. Jr., 126
Still, William, xv, 40–42, 43, 48–49, 52, 65, 91, 123–24
Stowe, Harriet Beecher, 52–53, 133
Sumner, Senator Charles, 104

Talbot County, Maryland, 3, 48
Taney, Chief Justice Roger B., 81–82
Tatlock, Helen, 118
Taylor, President Zachary, 28
Temporal lobe epilepsy (TLE), 10–11
Thomas, John, 124–25
Thompson, Anthony, 4–5, 12
Thompson, Dr. Anthony, Jr., 11–12, 74
Tobacco Stick, Maryland, 4
Topeka, Kansas, 81
Troy, New York, 88–89
Troy Vigilance Committee, 88–89
Truth, Sojourner, 65, 135, 137, 148
Tubman, Caroline, 37–38
Tubman, Harriet "Minty," xi–xiv; birth, 4; brain surgery, 140; childhood, 1–12; Civil War involvements, 95–111, 146; clairvoyance, 10–11, 22–23, 59–62, 79; daughters, 87–88, 93 nn.28, 30, 125–26; death, xiii, 142; on emancipation, 101–3, 109; escape from slavery, 21–22, 23–25; iconography of, 145–49; marriages, 17–18, 119–20; Moses reference, xiii, 35, 40, 49–50, 53 n.3; nursing career, 100, 107, 108–9; poverty of, 117–21, 124–25; on President Lincoln, 98–99, 101–2, 109; relationship with John Brown, 79–94; relationship with Thomas Garrett, 59–78; religious beliefs, 20, 38–39, 62, 131–32; rescues, xi–xiii, 29–30, 68–71, 88–89, 90–91; rewards for, 21, 35, 85, 90; women's rights involvements, 133–36

About the Authors

The late JAMES A. McGOWAN was editor of *The Harriet Tubman Journal* and author of several books, including *Station Master on the Underground Railroad: The Life and Letters of Thomas Garrett* (1977). His research on and contributions to African American history earned him the Angel of Philadelphia Award, presented by the William Still Foundation in 2003.

WILLIAM C. KASHATUS holds a doctorate in history from the University of Pennsylvania. A regular contributor to the *Philadelphia Inquirer*, Kashatus has written extensively on social justice issues. In 2002, he served as curator of Chester County (Pennsylvania) Historical Society's nationally acclaimed exhibit, "Just Over the Line: Chester County and the Underground Railroad."

www.ingramcontent.com/pod-product-compliance
Lightning Source LLC
Chambersburg PA
CBHW070444100426
42812CB00004B/1202